the
do-it-yourself
direct mail
handbook

the
do-it-yourself
direct mail
handbook

by Murray Raphel & Ken Erdman

RAPHEL PUBLISHING

Published by
Raphel Publishing
12 S. Virginia Avenue,
Atlantic City N.J. 08401

Book design by David Drotleff

Printed on recycled, acid-free paper.

Manufactured in the United States of America

ISBN 0-9624808-3-5

To those who own and operate a small business.
You're one of us.

So we share with you ideas, techniques and concepts of the most successful way to market, advertise and promote your business: **direct mail.**

MURRAY RAPHEL
KEN ERDMAN

Contents

PART TWO:
PRODUCING YOUR MAILER

FOREWORD

DIRECT MAIL IS basically a sales message delivered by mail.

It's a person-to-person, company-to-company, highly identified medium that can pinpoint its audience, personalize its message and measure the results through orders or inquiries returned to the sender. A medium that is truly the message!

The direct mail piece or package can employ every aspect of creative advertising. Copy can be long or short, graphics can include line drawings, photographs and full-color illustrations. Envelopes, letters and brochures can be designed in almost every imaginable size, shape and color. Specialities, gifts and premiums can be included to provide intrigue. The spoken word via microchips adds the dimension of sound, and even scented papers are available to take advantage of the sense of smell.

Direct mail may be the most versatile of all the media.

Through mailing list selection, both customers and prospects can be segmented into a wide variety of categories including age, sex, occupation, household income, auto ownership, business and charitable interests and even "lifestyle" as suggested through magazine subscriptions and other clues.

These highly defined segments of customers and prospects enable both the copywriter and artist to tailor their mailing to the particular interest of the audience selected. *Direct mail is* a targeted medium.

Unlike most other media, direct mail results are very measurable. Your mailing can seek orders, ask for inquiries or solicit contributions. By your returns shall you know your results. If you send out 10,000 letters and 1,000 customers respond, you have a 10 percent response — it's that simple.

Contrary to what many people mistakenly believe, direct mail makes a real contribution to the public, the Government and industry. Direct mail frequently eliminates the middle man, reducing the price of both goods and services. Direct Mail makes possible many charitable services through monies raised by mail solicitations.

The convenience of armchair shopping is made especially helpful to both the handicapped and the harried.

Businesses and the professions are kept constantly current on new products, processes, materials and services through business-to-business mail.

Politicians use direct mail to campaign and solicit campaign funds. They also use it to keep constituents informed. The Government has substantial budgets for direct mail as a very effective recruiting tool for all of the military services. Government supply facilities go to the mails regularly to seek bids and quotations for their every need.

And what about the Postal Service? Are those stories about "junk mail" really true?

In my book there's no such thing as "junk mail." All mail is valuable to someone. But some mail like some newspaper advertising or radio and TV commercials is disliked by some people, especially if the contents insult your intelligence or are an affront to one's reason. We humans enjoy *good* information no matter where it comes from. This is especially so if it's information that benefits us in some way.

What makes good information even more interesting when it comes by direct mail is the convenience of getting it directly into your home or office and of having the opportunity to read it on *your schedule* rather than on someone else's programmed schedule.

Now there is a how-to-do-it-yourself direct mail book for the small business: the banker, barber, beauty shop operator, manufacturer, retailer, the thousands of different types of small businesses that make up 80 percent of *all* businesses in the U.S.

Now they will know how to use a powerful advertising tool not only for their own customers but future customers as well.

Less than 10 percent of businesses in the U.S. have a customer data base. Since direct mail is a do-it-yourself medium, it makes sense to have a do-it-yourself book full of how-to-do-it instructions.

Direct Mail is an appreciated, effective, results-oriented medium. It's a medium many people can utilize *without* the aid of outside professional help. It's a medium that can produce significant results even on a do-it yourself basis. Direct mail really is advertising's best kept secret!

This publication now broadly shares this secret.

WILLIAM F. BOLGER
Former Postmaster General of the
United States of America

INTRODUCTION

IT ALL BEGAN WITH a phone call from Ken.

"Make believe you're a small business, Murray," he said.

"O.K." I said, "I'm a small business . . . "

It should be said up front that I am used to phone calls like this from Ken. Some people call and say "Hello." Others call and say who they are.

Not Ken. He begins the conversation in the middle of a story. You have to think fast, act smart and answer quickly.

"No," he said, "you're a bank and you have assets of between 100 and 500 million dollars."

"Sounds good to me," I said.

"No. On second thought, you're a supermarket."

"A supermarket? Well, O.K . . . "

"Perhaps you're a small- to medium-sized manufacturer."

"Hmmmmm, all right."

"No," he said, "you're a retailer!"

"Right on!" I answered because I am a retailer.

"And you do a million dollars or so every year in business. Now is that all right with you?

"Is *what* all right? Am I a bank? A supermarket, a manufacturer, a retailer? What's this all about?"

"This," he said, "is all about direct mail advertising. How you put together a direct mail program for your business. Any business Most are too small for an advertising agency. I recently read that most full service ad agencies require a minimum agency fee from their clients of $150,000. Or more."

"But all these businesses do other advertising, too," I reminded him.

"Yes," he agreed. "But you don't have to worry about doing your own newspaper ad because the newspaper sends a salesman. And so does the radio and the TV and the billboard company and the magazine and the high school athletic program book and t-shirts for the Little League. They all send around a salesman. But who's the direct mail salesman?"

Well, I had to admit, I didn't know of one . . .

"Exactly!" he cried, "because there isn't any. And yet how many times have I heard you say, 'Dollar for dollar, nothing returns as much business as direct mail'."

Well, if I said it, it must be right. But, I said, "I really don't want to be a . . . bank."

"Right," he said, "be what you are. A retailer who used direct mail to build a successful business. And a writer. Now, how about if we get together and write a book to help small businesses create result-producing do-it-yourself direct mail?"

"And how will our book be different from all the other direct mail books?" I asked.

"Easy," said Ken. "No complicated theory. No boring statistics. Just the easy basics. Lots of how-to-information. And case histories. And reference material, illustrations, places to go for help, all ready for the do-it-your-selfer."

"Great! How do we start?"

"By telling everyone all about direct mail. How it works. How they can do it. And how successful it is as America's best kept advertising secret . . ."

"Until now," I said.

"Right," said Ken. "Now make believe you're a small business . . . "

PART ONE:

PLANNING YOUR MAILER

Every human mind is a great slumbering power until awakened by a keen desire and by definite resolution to do.

— Edgar F. Roberts

1

Direct Mail: Familiarity breeds success!

IN THE BEGINNING . . .
a customer was treated as an individual.

There was no mass merchandising, marketing, advertising. The men and women who settled America brought their Old World techniques and talents to the new land. The tailor, the printer, the potter, the tinsmith, even the farmer, served customers one at a time.

As the country grew, most sales took place in small stores that sold small quantities to small groups of people. Face to face, one on one.

The customers returned because they were satisfied with the merchandise they bought and with the merchants from whom they bought it.

Shortly before World War II, there developed in this country a "mass market." Suddenly chain drugstores, chain supermarkets, chain shoe stores. chain everything began to appear serving a total market rather than an individual market.

As this mass marketing grew, so did the clamor for attention to this market.

Daily, the average person sees 300 or more advertising messages in print. They hear another three messages every few minutes they listen to the radio. They watch another five messages every fifteen minutes the TV is on. The clamor to capture attention becomes so loud it is amazing any message makes its way to anyone anytime.

What happened: Society moved from a personal society to an impersonal society. What was good for one became good for all. Suddenly the word "Occupant" appeared on mailings delivered to households all over the U.S. It made no difference who the occupant was, as long as there was an occupant.

But whenever a pendulum swings too far in one direction, there is a counterbalance set into motion. And the consumer wakes up one morning and resents being classified as "everyone" instead of "someone." The customer is ready, willing and anxious to respond to the merchant, manufacturer, business-man, baker, grocer who talks to him or her as an *individual.*

A recent survey said more people (63 percent) look forward to the mail than to such daily activities as watching TV, hobbies, eating dinner and sleeping.

When asked in a recent study what factors influenced a customer's decision to buy, 5,000 people said the first consideration was *confidence.* Second, quality. Third, selection. Fourth, service. *Price was fifth.* In fact, only 14 percent of the respondents listed price as the first reason for making a purchase or for selecting a business where they prefer to buy or shop.

That's why this book is important to you. It teaches you to recapture that original personal relationship through direct mail.

Direct mail is the most personal of all advertising.

It is a one-on-one, me-and-thee approach . . directed to a particular person at a particular address (not Occupant).

Dollar for dollar nothing will return as much to your business as direct mail.

Because you show the customer you care. Because you are talking to him and her as a person. Because it is simply going back to how it worked (and worked well) when . . .

In the beginning . . . a customer was treated as an individual.

HOW IT WORKS

Within the past few months I bought a $500 air conditioner, a life insurance policy, a $20,000 car and a $50 pair of shoes.

Following these sales, I heard from none of the businesses except my shoe salesman. He thanked me for coming in to buy and hoped I would "receive much comfort" and remember him the next time I wanted another pair of shoes. Or perhaps I had a friend who . . .

There's something wrong here.

I called each of the retailers (except the shoe store) and asked if they ever thought of writing thank-you letters after the sale. These are actual answers:

The air conditioner dealer: "I don't think we ever did that. Well, once in a while our financing company writes a letter to all the people they carry on their books." (What for? He wasn't sure.). "Listen, we know it's a good idea and I know you're going to ask why we don't do it, and the answer is, I guess we just never got around to it. There's so much to do in this business . . ."

The life insurance salesman: "I used to send thank-you letters. It was the best thing I ever did."

"But I stopped about eight or nine months ago. I'm so backed up with paperwork that I just don't have the time anymore. But I'll tell you something — from the customer's point of view it was terrific. I used to get a big response. I've got to get back to that sometime . . ."

The automobile dealer: "Are you kidding? Why that's the first thing we do. The day the car is delivered, the salesman sits down and writes a thank-you letter right away. Positively . . . "

Six months later there was still no letter.

What's happening?

Small business people — those are the people in about 80 percent of the businesses in this country — know the buzz words of successful businesses are "service" and "taking care of the customer."

Now, the smaller independently owned business can also show their customers they appreciate their business . . . in an advertising medium.

And this is where direct mail stands alone. Literally.

There is no confusion with other ads in the papers, on the radio or seen on TV. Because . . . direct mail *stands alone*. It carries your message to your customer with no competition.

A generally ignored fact of business: It is far, far easier to sell more to the customer you have than to sell a new customer.

How do you do that? Direct mail.

Our local florist recently celebrated its 100th year in business. The shop has one person responsible to send out reminders on who-sent-what-to-whom last year at this time and the florist will be glad to repeat the order if you simply call . . .

The customer contact that made the business successful through the years still works.

No wonder the business is still going strong after 100 years.

THE THREE WAYS
TO INCREASE YOUR BUSINESS
(And Only Direct Mail Works in All Three)

There are three ways you can increase your business.
And each of them involves customers:

1. Customers who are new to your business.
2. Customers who spend more money at your business.
3. Customers who come more often to your business.

Is there any advertising medium that brings in new customers, has present ones spend more when they arrive and makes them come more often?
There is: *Direct mail.*

TOOLBOX
FIFTY FACTS ABOUT DIRECT MAIL

1. Dollar for dollar, nothing returns as much to your business as direct mail.

2. For every 1,000 names in your database, you need one update per day.

3. Half your customers' names and addressses are inaccurate within three years unless updated.

4. Your customer list will return 2 to 10 times as much as a rented list.

5. Keep the person's TITLE (for addressing) and JOB (for selecting).

6. Only keep information that's important and that you'll maintain.

7. Sending the same offer to the same list returns 50% the first time response.

8. Renting a list for unlimited use for one year is usually only double the cost of a one time use.

9. Rent lists from publications where you advertise. And run ads and mailers at the same time!

10. Mail postcards first class. Cleans your list at NO cost.

11. Knowing ANYTHING about your customer is as important as knowing EVERYTHING about your product.

12. Average delivery of 3rd class mail: ten days!

13. Dimensional mailings (pop-ups) work! About 40% remember receiving this type of mailer six months later!

14. Mail ALL the names in your database at LEAST 4 times a year.

15. You'll receive 90 percent of your responses with two weeks.

16. Time to plan and send a direct mail campaign: 10 to 14 weeks.

17. Fulfill your customer's order within 48 hours of receipt.

18. Seminar mailings need up to 6 weeks for response.

19. Check with the post office BEFORE you send your mailing to see if it fits the rules.

20. Send copies of mailers to post offices of key zip codes telling them to "be on the lookout for . . . "

21. Personalize the response form. Increases results.

22. Hand write a "free" item on the response form. Increases results.

23. What's first read in a letter: The headline.

24. What's second read in a letter: The P.S.

25. Offer "yes" and "no" options. Reason: 25% of people that say "no" the first time will say "yes" the second time if you give them one more reason to buy.

26. Include a "Write names of people that would like to hear from us." Leave room for three names and addresses.

27. Ask: "Is this name and address correct?" Makes the reader involved.

28. The more ways to buy or respond, the more response.

29. Offer FAX, Fed Ex for quick response.

30. Order form summarizes the entire offer.

31. Write the order form FIRST. Then, write the offer.

32. Use surveys that can be completed in one minute.

33. Self mailers will not pull as well as a letter with envelope and a business reply card..

34. The more you use the word "you," the greater the response.

35. A separate reply device pulls better than one that has to be detached.

36. Use only white, ivory, ecru, or light gray paper for the message. Use colored stock for the reply card.

37. Best way to use labels: on the response card which shows through the window envelope (and has tracking codes).

38. Reply card is addressed to a person not to a company.

39. Customers buy confidence: Put number of years in business and big (BIG!) and easy to read Guarantee.

40. Watch the size of your mailers! Too big is too much postage.

41. The more you tell, the more you sell. Put as much in the envelope as you can without increasing postage.

42. Compare costs. Sending 1,000 letters first class costs about $100 more than sending them third class. And they're delivered faster *and they're delivered!*

43. Success is NOT "cost per unit mailed." Success is cost per lead. Or cost per sale.

44. More than half your future business comes from your present customers.

45. Multiple mailings are more effective than single mailings on a cost-per-lead basis.

46. Consider "piggy backing" with other non-competitive businesses. Cuts printing and postage costs.

47. Personal copy is more important than personalized copy.

48. The list is responsible for 40% of your success.
    The offer is responsible for 40% of your success.
    The creative is responsible for 20 % of your success.

48. The most powerful word in the English language is "FREE!"

49. Fear of loss is far more powerful than promise of gain.

50. TEST!

2

START WRITE NOW!

October 1

Dear Mrs. Brown,
 I sell good meat
and poultry.

Yours sincerely,
Albert Hawkins
Butcher

October 8

Dear Mrs. Brown,
 My customers can
be sure of prompt
delivery of good
meat and poultry.

Yours sincerely,
 Albert Hawkins
 Butcher

October 15

Dear Mrs. Brown,
 It doesn't cost
much.

Yours sincerely,
Albert Hawkins
Butcher

October 22

Dear Mrs. Brown,
 It doesn't cost
much to buy my
good meat and
poultry and have it
delivered.

Yours sincerely,
Albert Hawkins
Butcher

THE SERIES OF LETTERS on the previous page was actually mailed nearly a century ago to a group of home owners in a rural village in England. We are glad to report Mr. Hawkins, the butcher, did a land office business.

Why?

Because ... he wrote a personal letter to residents in his selling area, told them who he was, what he did and the advantages of buying from him. And reminded them again. And reminded them again. And reminded them again. And...

Writing a letter is the simplest form of direct mail. It is the definition of direct mail. The letter is *mailed directly* to your customer.

Direct mail shows your customers you care. You have taken the time to send your customers a personal message.

Direct mail is the medium that shows up your strong points: Friendliness, reliability, service and, most important, the amount of personal attention lavished on the customer.

Now, let's see how it works. And how you can do it starting... today.

It is not complicated. The easiest directions are the title of this chapter. **START WRITE NOW!** and write a letter to your customers as if you were writing a letter to yourself. Make it chatty, informal, comfortable, newsworthy.

That means you do *not* begin with the time-honored and boring sentences.

"In response to your letter of the 13th . . ."

"Pursuant to your notification of employment opportunities ..."

"I am in receipt of your letter of ..."

Begin with something to capture the reader's attention and interest. A story. A saying. An offer. Something that will make her stop ... and read.

It can be a headline like a story in the newspaper. It can be a question to make the reader wonder, "What's this all about?" It can promise a benefit if he keeps on reading.

Most importantly, ask yourself if your letter passes the **stop, look** and **listen** test.

STOP!

We once worked for a builder of houses. We went with him when he visited a piece of ground where he planned to build. We watched him walk over the ground. We heard him check for the location of utilities. We saw him work and re-work building plans.

A closet was sketched in, then erased. A bathroom was moved and re-moved on the blueprint. The final positioning of the house on the lot was changed and re-changed. There was the clearing of the title of the land.

One week later we said, "When do we start building?"

"Start building?" he replied. "That's the easy part."

Mailing the letter is the easy part. Knowing everything to do before the letter is mailed, the preparation, that is the tedious work. But . . . it's the work that makes your letter successful.

You can't write a letter until you first know what you want to accomplish.

First, decide what you want to do:

Sell merchandise? Introduce a new product? A new salesman? A new address? Tell someone who you are? Have someone vote for you? Ask questions for a survey?

Write down, in one sentence, what you want your finished letter to do.

Then, list the selling points and benefits. What are you doing? The same job the architect did a few paragraphs ago sketching plans for the finished product. This goes here. And that goes there.

Your letter, like a story, a play, a speech, has three parts:

A beginning.

A middle

An end.

It's really repeating the three-step formula:

• Say what you are going to say.

• Say it.

• Say what you said.

Your letter should follow these three steps in a logical sequence. *Your beginning* makes a dramatic statement ("What will happen to me if I read this?") *Your middle* explains in more detail what you just said ("Oh, so that's what they mean"). And reinforces your basic selling point ("Hmmm, look what happened to others who bought this"). *Your end* persuades and finally convinces ("Quick, where's my pen to fill in this order blank").

Having your letter follow a regular, organized presentation makes it easier for the customer to follow along. The clothing salesman does not show shirts then stop half-way through to bring socks. Then stop to show ties. Doesn't work. He sells the suit, then the shirt, then the tie, then the socks. One flows from the other.

This rhythm in face-to-face selling works in word-to-word selling. You make a statement ... then proceed to prove that statement.

But you cannot start until you first stop. Ask yourself:

WHAT DO I WANT THE READER TO DO AFTER HE READS THIS LETTER?

LOOK!

What does your letter "look" like?

If you write one long paragraph to fill each page, the letter is not too attractive to look at, much less read.

Keep your sentences short. Keep words to one or two syllables. Keep paragraphs to two or three sentences.

Avoid adjectives. Use action verbs. Eliminate unnecessary words that slow down the reader like "that"..."a"..."an."

Consider hand-written notes in the margin of your letter. They serve the same purpose as those little sub-headlines you see in printed copy. Gives the eye a rest from reading. Summarizes what you're about to read.

Use color. Sign your name in blue ink instead of black. What difference does that make? This: Your name will now stand out because the rest of the letter is in black type. And blue is an accepted color for signatures. Simple? Sure. And it works.

Use those figures on top of the number keys on your computer or typewriter. Push down the shift lock key and you'll discover ways to express amazement!!! And dashes to hook-things-together. Slashes for either/or choices. And another way to say &. You can whisper quietly in your letter (by saying something inside here) or yell louder by SAYING IT LIKE THIS.

The little dot can be a period ending a sentence like this. Or to keep you reading between sentences ... Like this . . . And this. Or to begin a series of reasons-why like:

- This reason here and
- Then this reason here.

LISTEN!

After you have finished writing your letter, read it aloud. "Listen" to it as though you were someone who received it rather than wrote it.

All the direct mail rule books say, "Write as though you were talking" or "Write a letter to your Aunt Minny."

That's all well and good and to be desired. But the truth is you want to capture the "feeling" of speaking. Don't actually write the way you talk. If so, each letter would run about 40 pages. The average person talks at the rate of 150 words a minute. One full page like this will take two minutes to read aloud. Five pages is ten minutes or more. That's a long time. You better have one good reason after another for them to keep on reading the pages.

Listen to the "sound" of your letter. Is your reader "comfortable" with what he is reading? Most of us have two languages. One for talking. Another for writing. We suddenly become academic English majors when we put pen to paper or fingers to computer. This may turn the reader off. If she is not comfortable reading, she will not like the letter or the product you want her to buy.

It also works in reverse: does your letter sound as though you like your reader? If so, it will come out in how you write. Be warm. Be friendly. Show the enthusiasm you have for your merchandise. Share the belief you have in the benefits they will receive. All this comes about in the words you use and how you use them.

Remember: Direct mail is a very special relationship between you and your customer. It is a me-and-thee approach. It is the two of you sharing some information. That can't happen unless you share common interests.

And even though you can achieve some nuances of speech by using the character keys on the computer, it is impossible for the printed word to gesture, roll its eyes, burst into laughter, cry or shrug its shoulders.

Listen to the arguments you make for buying in your letter. Would they convince you? Have you anticipated your readers' questions/ objections and come up with answers? Have you given them enough information to buy? Have you given them a guarantee that they must be satisfied or they receive their money back?

Have you given them a reason to act now? Quick! Today. And then have you given them several ways to buy? Cash. Charge. Time payment.

Never ask if they want to buy; offer different ways they *can* buy. And if you think of one more item you forgot to include, save it. There's a special place. One that has the highest "listening" potential in your letter. And that is *after* your signature. It is called the P.S.

After the headline, the P.S. is the best read part of a letter ("Aha! I wonder what they forgot to say in the letter?"). Make the P.S. a summary of what you said. Or include one more benefit. Or repeat the most important benefit. Or remind them of the deadline they must act by.

At this point, if you think all this is overwhelming, relax. The key words are: Are you natural?

Are you yourself?

Are you writing as if you were writing to *one* person and not to your hundreds or thousands or tens of thousands of customers?

Stop. Sit down. Decide what you're going to say. How you're going to say it. What you want to leave in and leave out.

Look. Does the letter "look" interesting to read?

Listen. How does it "sound" to you? Does it give a clarion call to buy?

WHAT WE HAVE HERE IS A FAILURE TO COMMUNICATE!

1

> John McIntyre, Plumber
> 1416 Main Street
> Middletown, New York
>
> Federal Bureau of Standards
> Washington, DC 20004
>
> April 1, 1992
>
> Gentlemen:
>
> I just wanted you to know that I found hydrocholoric acid is an excellent method for clearing clogged drain pipes. I thought you could use this information.
>
> Sincerely,
>
> John McIntyre, plumber

Make sure your letters are easy to understand. The exchange of letters on this page and the next page demonstrates the importance of communicating your message in easy-to-understand language.

2

> Federal Bureau of Standards
> Washington, D.C.
>
> John McIntyre, Plumber
> 1416 Main Street
> Middletown, New York
>
> Dear Mr. McIntyre:
>
> The efficacy of hydrocholoric acid is indisputable but the corrosive residue is incompatible with metallic performance.
>
> Claude T. Wilkinson
> Federal Bureau of Standards

1 John McIntyre, plumber, trying to be helpful.

2 Typical beaurocratic response.

3

> John McIntyre, Plumber
> 1416 Main Street
> Middletown, New York
>
> Federal Bureau of Standards
> Washington, DC 20004
>
> April 10, 1992
>
> Gentlemen:
>
> Thank you for your prompt reply. I am glad you approve using hydrochloric acid to clear clogged drain pipes.
>
> Sincerely,
>
> John McIntyre, plumber

3 Obviously, John didn't get the message.

4

> **Federal Bureau of Standards Washington, D.C.**
>
> **John McIntyre, Plumber**
> **1416 Main Street**
> **Middletown, New York**
>
> **Dear Mr. McIntyre:**
>
> **DON'T USE THE STUFF. IT EATS UP THE PIPES!**
>
> **Claude T. Wilkinson**
> **Federal Bureau of Standards**

4 Finally, a clear communication!

3

Everything Is at Sixes and Sevens

"EVERYTHING IS AT SIXES AND SEVENS" is an old-fashioned expression which means everything is confused and messy. But in direct mail "sixes and sevens" have a positive meaning. Because . . . there are *six* ways your business can use direct mail and *seven* rules for success.

The Six Ways to Use It
1. **Order by mail for a product or service.**
2. **Ask for a salesman to call.**
3. **Bring the reader to your place of business.**
4. **Do a simple advertising job on who you are.**
5. **Do some research.**
6. **Something other than a sale.**

Let's show you how each works:

1. Order by mail for a product or service. Nothing complicated about that. Just like the words say.
   • It can be a catalog you send to your customer.
   • It can be an item (or items) or service you include in a monthly statement.
   • It can be someone filling out a coupon in the newspaper and mailing it to you.

2. Ask for a salesman to call. You introduce a new piece of equipment. You show the product and whet the interest in a mailing piece. Now, give the prospect a chance to check a box, "Please have a salesperson call and tell me more about how this works."

Or . . . you receive a brochure from a manufacturer with fabric swatches enclosed and a letter saying why his merchandise is new and exciting. And then, "If you want to see the complete line and hear about our new plans simply call 800- . . ."

Or . . . you see a bank ad in major metropolitan dailies with the headline: "We make house calls." This is a half-step ahead of the "Fill out this application and mail it today . . ." (As in number one above.)

Or . . . a supermarket offers to deliver groceries. In this age of one-on-one marketing there is a vast audience of people out there who (1) don't like to shop for food; (2) are old and infirm and simply find it too difficult to shop for food, and (3) want someone to deliver sandwich trays for their party.

Your direct mailer can have all kinds of responses: by mail, by person or by phone.

3. Bring the reader to your place of business. This is how direct mail works for many businesses, professionals and most retail stores. Those who mail catalogs see customers come into their store *with* the catalog in their hand. The customer could have ordered by mail but decided instead to see the merchandise first hand. Live. In person. Ready to buy.

This is also the best example of direct mail's greatest strength. You let your customer know something no one else knows. Something just between the two of you. This is why we say, "'tis far, far easier to sell more to the customer you have than to sell a new customer."

Use direct mail to bring your customers to your store, your business, your service, your trade show because you offer them something special because well, *they* are something special: Your customers.

4. Do a simple advertising job on who you are. Some call this "institutional" advertising, letting the potential customer know who you are and what you do. Nothing wrong with that. When you have just opened for business, it is a good idea to let the local folks know you are in business and where you are and what you have for them to buy.

If you are a bank, send a mailer to the local businesses where you plan to open your branch bank.

If you are a supermarket, send weekly mailers to the people living in your shopping area. Tell them you have arrived, and what you have to sell. Don't forget to include some coupons to bring them in. (The mailboxes in Finland are packed every week with advertisements from competitive food stores).

5. Do some research. Are you what you think you are? Or something else instead? One way to find out: Ask your customers.
It can be a simple "We want to serve you better" questionnaire where you list all the pro and con adjectives and ask the customers to pick and choose. ("Which adjective best describes our business to you'? Check one: ❏ friendly, ❏ courteous ❏ goes out of its way to help, ❏ just the opposite of all those."

Or you are thinking of taking in new merchandise. Would your customer buy these items? Ask them ahead of time.

Or: What would your customers like you to carry or make that you are not presently carrying or making?

Or: You may simply want to find out more about your customer. Either (a) who they are, or (b) what they want. We tend to think our customers are the same as we are-the same demographics (where we live, how much we earn), psychographics (what we think about), like to jog, have a mortgage, three kids, and two cars.

Sorry, not true.

There is a general description of who/what/where your customers are and it is probably not the same as who/what/where you are. It is important you know. It is best if *they* tell you.

6. Something other than a sale. You make an announcement about your business' address. Or new employee(s). Or a seminar you are conducting. A reason to vote for you (or your friend) in the upcoming election. A request for a contribution to your favorite charity.

Direct mail is a selling tool. But it does not have to be merchandise. It can be a thought, a concept, a commitment to a person or organization.

How about a "thank you" *after* the sale. Neiman-Marcus employees jot customers a little note thanking them for shopping with them. It s remembered and talked about to others.

Important: Each of these six reasons-for-using tells the customer more about you and your product or service and reinforces your image in the community.

Most people in business assume since they have been in business for so many years that everyone knows who they are, what they do, when they are open, where they are and why people seek them out. Wrong.

We call this the "Curse of the Assumption." You assume everyone knows who you are and what you do. But one out of five people in the community in which you live change their address every year.

One of the most famous ads in American advertising history is called "The Angry Man Ad." (See illustration next page). It was published by McGraw-Hill and selected by *Advertising Age* as one of the ten best institutional ads of all time. It shows a heavy-set scowling executive sitting in a chair and staring at you. Next to him are these sentences:

I don't know who you are.
I don't know your company.
I don't know what your company stands for.
I don't know your company's record.
I don't know your company's reputation.
I don't know your company's customers.
Now . . . what is it you wanted to sell me?

We *assume* because we know who we are, where we work and our spouse knows and our children know and our parents know and our nieces and nephews and cousins know — well then, everyone knows. Not true.

But direct mail is a constant reminder to your customer not only of who you are but that you are still doing business at the same stand

"I don't know who you are.
I don't know your company.
I don't know your company's product.
I don't know what your company stands for.
I don't know your company's customers.
I don't know your company's record.
I don't know your company's reputation.
Now — what was it you wanted to sell me?"

MORAL: Sales start **before** your salesman calls—with business publication advertising.

McGRAW-HILL MAGAZINES
BUSINESS•PROFESSIONAL•TECHNICAL

*Reproduced by permission of McGraw-Hill Magazines.

in the same place with the same kind of products or services.

L. L. Bean of Freeport, Maine saw their clothing, shoe and camping business increase tenfold simply because they increased their mailings to their customers from twice a year to *every* month. They discovered their customers did not want to buy the merchandise only when L. L. Bean thought they wanted to buy the merchandise. The customers wanted the merchandise all year long.*

O.K., now that you know *what* Direct Mail will do for your business, *how* should you do it?

We have read, examined, digested dozens of rules and secrets and reasons why direct mail works (See Toolbox: The Formula to End All Formulas at the end of this chapter) .

Nearly forty years ago, Edward Mayer, Jr., one of the earliest writers and lecturers on direct mail said there were seven cardinal rules for direct mail success:

1. **Establish an objective.**
2. **Say what it does for the reader.**
3. **Make the layout and copy fit.**
4. **Address correctly.**
5. **Make it easy to take action.**
6. **Repeat.**
7. **Test.**

Let's take a closer look at each rule:

1. Establish an Objective.
What do you want your mailing piece to accomplish?

It is amazing how many mailing pieces never tell you what they want you to do. This information should be up front. Are you introducing a new product? Asking for an order? Want a salesman to come and explain in more detail?

Once you know what you are trying to do, the writing of the mailer will follow that direction.

* Write for a copy of L. L. Bean's catalog, Freeport, Maine 04033

2. Say What It Does for the Reader.

Direct mail answers this question far more effectively than any other advertising because it is the most personal of all advertising. Let's show you how it works:

You meet an attractive woman (or man). You ask her out for dinner. You have a good time. The next day you write her a letter saying, "Thank for an exciting and thoroughly enjoyable evening. I hope we can do it again soon. I really enjoyed being with you."

She reads your note and thinks it was rather nice of you to say those nice words and tucks the note in her pocketbook.

Now, let's assume instead of sending her a note, you take out an ad in her local newspaper. Your headline says "An open message to . . ." with her name. The ad has the same words as the letter.

Would she be complimented . . . or embarrassed?

Or . . . you contact the radio station in her home town and have the radio announcer read the same message over the air. Would she be complimented . . . or embarrassed? Her friends could easily read other meanings into the same words.

She is offended! She thinks you are terrible! She is embarrassed to see her friends!

What happened? When you wrote the same words in a letter, her reaction was warm and positive. When you put it out for all the world to see, her reaction was cold and negative.

Why? Because direct mail forms an emotional bond between you and your customer unattainable in any other advertising medium.

In fact, your customers look forward to receiving mail from you. Few will pick up the morning paper and look for your ad or twist the dial trying to hear your commercial ad. But most will open, read and often act on your ad if they receive it in the mail.

If a customer of ours does *not* receive a mailer that they know others have received, the reaction is immediate and irritated. A phone call comes wanting to know why we left them off the list. We apologize, blame the post office or the mailing house . . . all to no avail. We have discriminated against them, and they are mad!

It happened to the First National Bank of Wilmette, Illinois. They put together a five week direct mail program. Every Thursday morning the residents of Wilmette would receive a message from the bank advertising one of their products or services.

One week it listed all the services the bank offered. The next week it announced the bank's special hours. The fifth and last week summarized the four services and included a calling card from a bank officer.

That ended the campaign.

Or so thought the bank.

On the Thursday morning of the sixth week, the bank's phones started ringing early and continued all day long. They had a record number of incoming calls that day. When someone from the bank answered, they would hear a voice on the other end of the line saying, "I didn't get any mail from the bank today. How come?"

People like to receive mail!

3. Make the Layout and Copy Fit.

"You don't wear a tuxedo to the beach," said writer/lecturer Ed Mayer "and you don't wear a bathing suit to a formal dinner."

If you are advertising men's work clothes, the mailing piece will not have a soft feminine look.

Your mailing must have a mood and feeling and image and look that is you.

"Every advertisement that you run is an investment in yourself," says advertising expert David Ogilvy. And it's true.

The typeface you choose. The color you select. The artist you employ. Each of these must work together to come up with a total concept the customer associates with you and your business.

Example: supermarkets print four-color tabloids they mail to all the households in their area. But most supermarket ads look so much alike, the customer is not sure where the mailing piece came from until they look at the name.

That was the problem facing Charley Braun in his Food Ranch supermarket in Mud Lake, Idaho. (Yes, there is a Mud Lake, Idaho.)

For years Charlie did the same advertising as his competitor: the four-color 8-page tabloid mailed to every "Occupant" in his home town. The people received these mailers along with the mailers from all the other stores. Impact was small. So he tried something different. One Thanksgiving he mailed an 8 1/2" x 11" sheet of paper to his customers with food specials typewritten on one side. The other side said this was his "No frills" advertising. The rest of the page was left blank for children to draw pictures of turkeys and bring the sketches to the store for a prize.

Sales jumped 80 percent over previous "professional" mailings.

"When they receive one of my new mailers," says Charlie, "they know it's from me and not someone else."

4. Address Correctly.

This rule has two meanings.

The first is as the words say: Make sure you send your mailer to the correct address. (Remember that one out of five people in your town moves every year.) And . . . it also means to spell the name correctly. People dislike having their name misspelled.

We received a selling letter beginning, "Dear Rapahel Murray." Backwards. And misspelled.

Followed by this clever opening line:

"I don't need to tell you how important first impressions can be." We agreed and threw that one away!

Ken Erdman once signed a "request for more information" coupon and reversed the name and address lines. He put his city (Philadelphia) on the line set aside for "name."

To this day, Ken Erdman receives mail addressed to Phil A. Delphia and of course, beginning, "Dear Phil..."

Addressing correctly also calls attention to two key ingredients necessary for a successful direct mail piece:

I . The list.

2. The offer.

If you have an excellent product but advertise it to the wrong people ... you will have few sales.

If you have an excellent mailing list but advertise an item not applicable to this group . . . you will have few sales.

What does that mean?

This: If you have a list of senior citizens and you mail them an offer for acne medication ... you have few sales. (Good list, bad offer.)

This: If you are selling retirement homes at a low price and you sent the offer to newlyweds ... you will have few sales. (Good offer, bad list.)

Most people in business have a list of their customers. Milt Smolier, past president of the mailing house Names Unlimited, said, "If you have a mailing list of customers, you're in the direct mail business."

The direct mail professionals call that information a "database." Fine. What it is is a list of your customers' names and addresses. The ones who know you, who shop with you and (most importantly) will open and read what you send them.

Companies sending out mailings to "Occupant" are satisfied if they receive a 1/2 of 1 percent return. (Translation: If they mail out 100,000 mailers and 500 customers show up to buy, they are happy.)

But businesses who mail to their own customers show consistent returns of 5-20 percent or *more*.

5. Make It Easy to Take Action.

Always include a "response mechanism." That means the customer can fill it out and send it back to you by simply dropping a card or business-reply envelope into the mailbox. (Yes, you pay the postage. Would you pay a few pennies to have a customer come in your front door or call on your phone ready to buy?)

Give your customers *different* ways they can buy.

The more choices you give them, the greater response.

This is a variation of a selling technique you use every day in your business called the "Not If But Which" method. You never offer a customer one shirt and ask him if he wants to buy it. You offer several and say, "Which one do you like?"

Or a choice of cars or insurance programs or computers or whatever you sell.

And so, you let your customer pay you by cash. Or check. Or charge. Or their choice of credit cards. Or calling this 800 number. Or by simply pulling off the "Yes" or "No" sticker and putting the one they want on the label or return card.

Now-why do businesses *pay* to find out who does *not* want to buy as they do when you send back the "No" sticker?

Because you want the customer *involved* with you. By taking off the "No" sticker, putting it on the reply card and writing their name and address, they show they are interested ... but not convinced.

Now that you have them involved, how do you make them feel committed?

Here's how: write back to the ones who said "No." State all the advantages one more time and then give them one *more* reason to buy.

Tests show about one out of four customers who say "No' the first time around will say "Yes" the second time around.

Always, always, always, always offer a GUARANTEE with your mailer. They must be satisfied or they can have their money back.

6. Repeat!

McGraw-Hill published a survey that says it takes a salesman an average of five calls to make the first sale.

When you add up to the approximate $300 per sale cost, this is a lot more expensive than five direct mail pieces to the same customer.

Very few salespeople make the sale the first time around. Even the best often use the first call to find out information they need for the second call.

Persistence is a key to effective selling. Which was certainly the quality of the tie salesman who called on us for four years without making a sale. "When are you going to stop coming to see us?" we asked him one time. He looked, paused, then said, "Depends on which one of us dies first."

Chase Manhattan bank mailed letters asking if you wanted to borrow money. There was a deadline stamped on the letter showing the latest day you can take the Chase Advantage of this offer.

The deadline passes. You have lost out. But, no ... wait! Here is another letter from Chase. Well, really the *same* letter. But where the deadline date was, it is now crossed out in red with the phrase "Extended until ..." and a **new** date a week away.

Another technique is called "The Publisher's Letter" because it began with book clubs. (It's also called a "Lift Letter" because it lifts the rate of response.)

How it works: Within your mailing piece include a folded-over note. On the outside it has a phrase similar to this: "Do not open unless you have decided *not* to buy."

When your customer opens this little note, she sees a short memo from the president of your company or a testimonial of a well-known person. Who simply can't believe she is not buying the product. And here's one more reason why she should ...

"Publisher's Letters" in quantities of a few thousand cost less than a penny apiece to print and can increase a return by as much as 10 percent. That's 10 percent *additional.*

(Example: if you were normally having a 5 percent return, adding this little reminder increases your return to 5.5 percent. Or 10 percent more.)

7. Test!

This is the one unique characteristic that belongs to direct mail advertising.

You do not have to spend money on printing and postage of massive mailings until you first test to see the probable results.

Direct mail is the only form of advertising you can test for results. Imagine asking the newspaper if your ad can be in the paper but delivered only to certain sections of your community.

Imagine telling the radio or TV salesman to broadcast your message only into certain sections of town.

"Impossible," they say. "Can't do it," they would reply.

But with direct mail you can pinpoint the customer you want, where you want and as many as you can. Or as few.

And it's measurable!

You know the results almost immediately.

If you send out 10,000 letters and 1,000 customers respond, you have a 10 percent response.

How do you *really know how* many people read the paper or heard the radio and responded?

And will your newspaper guarantee you one percent of their total circulation will respond to your ad?

If they will, place *all* your money in that newspaper.

But they will not. They cannot.

Yet you can receive a response of 10 or 20 percent or *even more* from your own mailing list, from your own customers.

In this book you will read of businesses receiving as much as *80 percent return.*

(For more information on testing see Chapter 15.)

It's been said direct mail is a *what* medium not a *why* medium. If you send out 10,000 letters and you receive 1,000 orders you know what happened. You had a 10 percent response. But you don't necessarily know why. Wouldn't it be simple and easy if there was a magic formula for success?

We went to some of the top experts in direct mail and asked if they would give us their Secret Formula ...

TOOLBOX

THE FORMULAS TO END ALL DIRECT MAIL FORMULAS

Ponce de Leon left St. Augustine unhappy because he could not find the Formula for Everlasting Youth. Dr. Jekyll had a bad lunch when he whipped up a formula only to find it changed his Hyde. Those looking for the formula to make both ends meet soon discover what happens when you burn the candle at both ends.

Throughout history, people looking for the quick fix, easy solution and magic formula have, more often than not, been disappointed.

But the search continues in all walks of life, business and ... direct mail.

Is there a magic formula, once used, that guarantees success?

Are there words, phrases, concepts, once put together, that will bring in the crowds, ring the register, fill the bank account?

Is there a way to guarantee success once the pen is put to the paper, the fingers on the typewriter, the floppy disk in the computer?

Well, yes.

And then again, no.

There are books written, speeches given and seminars conducted on the never ending search for why ... why does direct mail work when it *does* work?

We contacted some of the best known direct mail experts around the world. We asked them for their exclusive formula. Would they share this secret with us?

Amazingly, they all said Yes.

It's off to the lab for those not-so-secret formulas.

AIDA

Attention, **I**nterest, **D**esire, **A**ction

This is seen in almost every text and best remembered by Verdi's opera of the same name: *Aida.*

Earliest publication seems to be in 1920 by Cyril Freer, advertising manager of the Daily Mail, according to Drayton Bird, United Kingdom DM expert. (Here in the colonies, credit is given to E. K. Strong in his 1925 book, *The Psychology of Selling.)* Freer's book, *The Inner Side of Advertising* said a good sales letter should include:

"The opening which should attract the reader's *Attention* and induce him to read.

"The description and explanation should hold their *Interest* by causing him to picture the proposition in his or her mind.

"The argument should create the *Desire* for the article offered for sale. And ...

"The climax which makes it easy for the reader to order and assures that *Action* by causing him to act at once."

KISS

Keep **I**t **S**hort and **S**imple

Short sentences. Short paragraphs. Words of one and two syllables. All easily understood and quickly acted upon. The simplest direct mail package seems to, more often than not, outpull the more complicated packages.

(A variation of this phrase came from the frustrated head of an ad agency who could not convince his Ph.D. English copywriter that intellectualism in writing did not sell merchandise. In frustration, he yelled out his own interpretation of the formula saying, "Keep It Simple, Stupid!")

P P P P

Picture, Promise, Proof, Push

It was nearly thirty years ago that Henry Hoke, grandfather of the publisher of *Direct Marketing* magazine, wrote a booklet for the Bureau of Business Management at the University of Illinois. The title: *How to Use the Mails for Sales.*

The formula Hoke gave us then (that still works today) is this one:

Start your message by having the customer *picture* your offer. You then *promise* this picture will become a reality if they simply buy your product. *For proof* here is what other folks just like you say about how much they enjoy this merchandise. And so, hurry, quick, now, at-once, the *push* is on for you to order.

R F M

Recency, Frequency, Monetary

These are often called the three most important factors in customer information. The trio were the first to find their way onto computer floppy discs.

They mean what they say. Recency is first because it tells you the most recent date the customer bought from you.

The next, Frequency, tells you how often they buy, the more frequent, the more loyal, the more valuable.

The last, Monetary, tells you how much they spend either on the latest order or during the time they have been on your list.

OK, those are the best known and most used formulas.

Now, are there other formulas out there, kept hidden and guarded through the years by some of the best-known practitioners of our craft?   And, would they, upon request, reveal their sources?

The answer was yes and yes.

There were other formulas out there. And the winners were willing to share.

Let us remind you up front that *books* have been written on direct mail formulas. In picking and choosing these, we set the criteria of nonduplication and, for the most part, from writers working today with consistent records of success.

Here they are in alphabetical order.

ED BURNETT
Ed Burnett Consultants

Ed came up with his version of the Marx brothers: Dido, Gigo, Nino and Rafo. He says the computer world has spawned a whole new list of formulas to be observed and paid attention to:

They include:

DIDO *D*uplication *I*n, *D*uplication *O*ut

GIGO *G*arbage *I*n, *G*arbage *O*ut

NINO *N*ot *I*n, *N*ot *O*ut

RAFO What you do when you forget to NINO. You go back and *R*esearch *A*nd *F*ind *O*ut.

In other words: the computer only gives back to you what you give it. Not far different from the age-old dictum of you only get out of something what you put into it ...

RAY CONSIDINE
Considine & Associates

The Salesman from the West reminds us there is nothing that successfully replaces his *Four-mula for Success* with customers or clients.

Like a four-a-day vitamin schedule: take four of one, or one of each, or any mix. "It always works," says this direct marketing doctor.

Prescription: Four Notes (handwritten). Four telephone calls (brief). Four PCs (no, no, not IBMs but *P*ersonal *C*ontacts asking for referrals). Four AFTOs (in itself, *another* formula "*A*sk *F*or *T*he *O*rder").

The secret, Raymond says, is there is no secret. Direct marketers who are successful always stay in touch with their best customers.

KEN ERDMAN
Co-author

Not to be outdone, co-author, Ken wanted his "Chicken Pox" formula included. It works like this: after you have written your letter or copy, go over it carefully and draw a red circle around all of the personal pronouns; I, we, us, ours, my. Then look for exaggerated words; biggest, best, most, etc. Then if your work seems to suffer from chicken pox you need a quick cure.

Change the red-circled pronouns to the words "you" or "yours" and try to tone down the exaggerated claims.

Look again. If the rash has disappeared, you are on your way to healthy copy.

FREEMAN GOSDEN
Smith-Hemmings-Gosden

"I don't use the formulas 'cause I can never remember the letters ...", says Freeman Gosden. But he *does* remember *numbers!* His most successful: the 40-40-20 formula.

40% marketing: Who you are. What product or service you offer. What is the price or "deal."

40% audience: The right list (from the more than 35,000 available). Advertising in the right media at the right time.

20% creativity: Copy. Theme. Format. Graphics. Paper. Envelopes. Color. Postage. And more.

His conclusion: get the first two right and the third falls into place.

ROSE HARPER
The Kleid Company

The president of The Kleid List Company admits she has been trying to create a winning formula for a long time. She called her staff together and had them vote. Their choice: T A P.

They agreed on the initials. But not on the words. The two choices take your pick): *T*est, *A*nalyze, *P*roject. Or *T*est, *A*nalyze, *P*rogress.

RICHARD HODGSON
Writer, Speaker on Direct Marketing Techniques

The man who wrote the book on successful mail order advertising says there are two Hodgson formulas:

1. Don't use formulas.

2. Hire someone who knows enough not to use a formula.

Copy written by a formula is like a horse created by a committee. It turns out to be a camel, says Hodgson.

He admits all the experts have formulas, and since he is an expert, he does say there are four key words that form the cornerstone of successful direct marketing. Each of these words "should be preceded by the adjective, 'perceived,'" says Hodgson. "The real facts are not often as important as what the potential customer perceives to be the facts." Here are the four words:

1. *Availability:* Does the reader think your product is not easily accessible in a nearby shop?

2. *Authority:* Testimonials from well-known people/organizations. History of how long you've been in business. A reason-why the reader thinks your product is superior.

3. *Value:* The customer must feel they are receiving something of value for them. This has nothing to do with your mark-up. But rather what the merchandise means to them in terms of their needs.

4. *Satisfaction:* The well-known "guarantee" you see in all the direct mail catalogs.

IAN KENNEDY
K&D Bond International Pty Limited

Our friend from Australia and member of their Direct Marketing Hall of Fame plays the percentages. He says success is List 100, offer 50 and creative 10. Brilliant creative and strong offers will never survive the wrong audience.

ED NASH
President, Ed Nash Direct

"Aha," says Ed, "so *that's* how formulas come about. People like me don't want to be left out of books by people like you..."

He likes the AIDA formula as taught to him by Vic Schwab. But his personal favorite ("and revealed here for the first time") in his "Five S Formula": Stop 'em/Show 'em/Seduce 'em/Satisfy 'em/Sell 'em.

Stop 'em: with a headline to separate prospects out.

Show 'em: words and no words: pictures, people, images, all reinforcing the headline.

Seduce 'em: emotional needs, fantasy, self-image.

Satisfy 'em: an offer the reader can't refuse.

Sell 'em: Ask for the order. (See AFTO under Considine.)

PIERRE PASSAVANT
Passavant Seminars & Consulting

It's not *exactly* a formula, says international lecturer and consultant Passavant, but it works! He calls it the Escalator of Promotion Intensity (EPI). His point: There is a difference between "ordinary" and "extraordinary" offers. "That difference," says Pierre, "is often in the intensity of the promotional elements used. The more the intensity, the higher the response potential." And then adds, cautiously, "most of the time . . . "

JERRY REITMAN
Vice President, Leo Burnett

It was Henry Hoke who gave this advice for newcomers in direct mail copywriting: "Blue pencil the first paragraph." His point: It usually takes a new writer that long to get to the point. He felt beginners tended to approach a sales proposition with the bullpen approach, taking a few paragraphs to warm up.

Jerry Reitman says almost the same thing with this WIDDWO formula. Translation: *W*hen *I*n *D*oubt, *D*o *W*ith*o*ut."

One more from Jerry: QTBP = *Q*uality *I*s *T*he *B*est *P*olicy.

JOHN FRASER ROBINSON
Great Britain

Our creative friend from England has a "GOLDEN" Strategy.
Grab attention
Open strongly
Lead logically
Demand action
Encourage response
Need it now

JAMES ROSENFIELD
President, Buchanan/Vinson/Rosenfield Direct

Jim's METHOD reads from top to bottom:
   Motivate
   Elucidate
   Tangibilize
   Humanize
   Over-simplify
   Direct!
Why not? If METHOD works for Actor's Studio graduates, why not for Jim Rosenfield?

JOE SUGARMAN
JS&A Sales

"My formula is called the 'Slippery Slide' Theory," says top copywriter Sugarman.

"Simply stated, if you climb on a slide that is slippery, you are going to slide all the way to the bottom unable to stop. That's the way I do my ads. Once you start reading them, you can't stop. Then, if you're a good salesman, you're going to get your message across on the ride down."

Joe built his famous seminars around this basic theory.

JOAN THROCKMORTON
Joan Throckmorton Inc.

Leading direct mail consultant Throckmorton believes in the "Underlying Law of Creativity in Direct Response Advertising." Whatever you say, however you say it, however you present it, ask first: "Does this make sense to the customer?"

WALTER SCHMID
International Direct Marketing Symposium

Walter has seen the world's experts perform for more than twenty years on his international stage in Montreux.

After hearing and seeing them all, he simply says, "I think your list is complete." He adds, "Should I run across another formula, I will let you know."

We're going to write Walter back and say, "Don't tell us. This is it. No more." As Carlyle said, "It is now almost my sole rule of life to cleanse myself of all formulas."

4

I'VE GOT YOU ON MY LIST

WE VISITED A NEARBY supermarket that needed more sales. We asked if they had a mailing list. They said no.

We asked if they kept names of customers from contests, sweepstakes and in-store continuity programs. They said no.

We then asked if they issued courtesy cards so customers could cash checks.

"Sure."

Well, we asked, "isn't that a mailing list?"

"No," they answered. That was only the names of their courtesy card holders ...

What happened?

The store *had* a mailing list and did not know they did. This situation is not uncommon. Most businesses have lists of customers on their charge accounts. They have names and addresses of best customers kept by sale people. They have alteration tags, layaways, call-back records, quotations, special order books and service calls. The problem is ... no one thinks of these names as anything but ... names.

But they are something far more important. They are names of the people who know you, buy from you and are interested in what you have to say/sell to them in the future. They are the nucleus of your very own data base. Your mailing list.

THE LIST is one of the two must-have ingredients for successful direct mail. (The other important part is THE OFFER. See chapter 5.)

Begin a customer list. Now. Today. At once. Think of all the places you have customer names. Start with the ones we mentioned a few

paragraphs above. Put these names, addresses and zip codes on 3"
x 5" cards in a little box or enter them into a computer. Let them
accumulate. You will see they will quickly multiply as the days go
by. Soon a few hundred names become a few thousand.

If you have a service or professional business or if you are a
wholesaler, your clients are your mailing list.

If you have a store, print up 3" x 5" "I want to receive mail from
…" paper slips. Very simple. Very inexpensive. Place them on all
your checkout counters. Do not worry about the cashier(s) taking a
lot of time gathering all this information at check-out time. They
don't. Here's how it works:

Your customer brings her package to the check-out counter. Your
cashier says, "We have a special mailing list. It is only for our regular
customers. Just fill this out and you'll receive some exciting notices
we mail only to special people like you …"

They will almost tear the pen out of the cashier's hand in their
hurry to sign. Everyone wants to be "in the know." You want to offer
them something no one else knows about and are they interested?

Oh, yes.

Gathering names is habit-forming, just like eating peanuts. Once
you start you will find you cannot stop. But you have to *start*. You
have to set the example yourself and others in your business will
follow. Ask everyone at the end of the day. "How many people did
we [you?] sign on our mailing list today?"

At this early stage do not worry if someone signs up twice. You
will catch their name later. (We'll show you how.)

Right from the start, you might want to be a little more
sophisticated in your name gathering. Perhaps you have a checklist
on your sign-up list of what they are buying. A list of people buying
a particular brand. We have a list of names of customers who buy
only one designer's clothing. We mailed them something *every*
month just from this designer. Our return averaged 20 percent! The
per unit sale was more than $100. Very effective. We simply added
this designer's name to the sign-up list.

If the customer bought this merchandise, we checked it off at the
point of sale on the list they filled out.

Remember this simple rule: If a customer spends money with you, that name goes on the mailing list.

Not the shoppers and browsers and let's-kill-some-time-here folks. The ones who actually spend: They are customers.

Definition of a customer: Someone who spends one dollar with you at least one time in your store or business. Now your customer may also be a customer of your competition. But they know who you are and have shown enough faith to spend money at least once.

This is the customer you want. Because:

'TIS FAR, FAR EASIER TO SELL MORE TO THE CUSTOMER YOU HAVE THAN TO SELL A NEW CUSTOMER.

If that's true (and it is) then how do we have that customer come back and back and back and back *ad profitum?*

We could advertise in the newspaper and radio and TV and magazines and church bulletins. But that's advertising to *everyone.* We want you to advertise to *someone.* That someone whose name you now have on your *list.*

O.K., you've started. You put out slips for people to sign up for your list. You assign someone to go over any area of your business that might have customers' names and addresses. You copy those on your 3" x 5" cards. File the cards alphabetically making it easy to look up and see whether or not a new name is listed twice. Or, if you have a computer, you enter the names and addresses into a simple mailing list program.

You can maintain your own list for a few thousand names. You are now ready to (choose one):

1. Write or type or print labels for small mailings.
2. Write or type or print addresses on envelopes from names and
   addresses on cards.

When the list grows bigger, contact a local mailing house. They will put all your names on a computer for you and print labels or the name directly on your mailing piece.

They will print your names. And/or they will code the names when they put them in the computer so if you want just *certain* names to mail to certain people who buy just certain merchandise or use a certain service, fine!

You checked off that information on the original sign-up list, remember? Now, you tell your mailing house to simply pull only these names. The computer is smart. If you told the computer in the beginning about those names, it will tell you back.

The mailing house also performs a service called Merge & Purge. Sounds like a South American coup. What it really is: computers have a way of "scanning" each new name they receive. If it "looks" the same as one they already have with the same address, they simply "purge" that name out ... all the while they are "merging" the other names in.

But that's down the road.

First: collect the names. Count them. Do you have 1,000? Great. Time to start.

Here's why: Dr. Russell Conwell gave a speech called "Acres of Diamonds" more than 100 years ago.

The speech was so much in demand, he told and retold it thousands of times throughout the United States eventually making more than $6 million which he used to found Temple University in Philadelphia, Pennsylvania.

The theme: Why are you trying so hard to find new places to make your fortune when the fortune is waiting right in your own backyard? If you want your sales to increase, if you want your business to grow, if you want more ringings of your register, practice a proven, successful and winning formula called, Keep In Touch which, for the purpose of this chapter, we condense to the initials KIT.

Think about it.

If you have a bank, and customers have a checking account, why don't they have a savings account? And if they have a checking and savings account, why not an IRA? And if they have a checking and savings account, and an IRA, why not a loan? And if they have a checking and savings account, an IRA, and a loan, why not ... well, you get the idea.

If you have a supermarket, you know your average customer spends about $60 a week with you. And, therefore (say you), they cannot spend anymore. Makes sense, until you see the same customer coming out of a nearby convenience store with another bag of groceries. These are not only the same groceries you have in your store, but they are groceries that probably cost more in the convenience store.

If you have a clothing store you know what your customers can afford to spend, based on their past experience with you, their job, and the size of their family. And you are content to have a good triple figure sale at the beginning of a season. You conclude that they spend as much as they can afford. Until you see them come out of another store in the nearby shopping mall with another shopping bag full of clothing similar to what you sell in your store.

So you can increase sales to your current customers. But, remember, only a small percentage of your customers give you a large percentage of your business.

The philosopher Pareto (1848-1923) was the first to tell us about the 80-20 rule. Pareto said 80 percent of your sales are brought to you by only 20 percent of your customers. Fund raisers for major political campaigns or charity drives say, "Yes, we want a lot of names to establish the bandwagon approach."

"Everybody's contributing. Don't you want to be among the bunch?"

But their real effort, their intense drive, their pinpoint marketing is keyed to the much, much smaller group (the 20 percent) who wind up giving the lion's share (80 percent) of the money.

Sometimes the figures are even more dramatic than that. Roger Horchow in his book *Elephants in Your Mailbox* writes that when he first started his mail order catalog, "the rent-payers were ten customers who were spending over $10,000 a year with us."

Competition gets tougher as new products, ideas and stores spring up around you; remember, if business is good, it's because you are buying well and selling well. You are doing something right.

And if business is bad, it's not the weather. It's not the economy. It's not the location. It's you. You are doing something wrong. Somebody is buying something somewhere. Your job is to figure out how to have customers spend a larger part of their disposable dollars in your store, buying your merchandise.

This philosophy is best practiced by a major association of meat packers. This association says that a stomach has only so much capacity. The goal of the packers is for meat to take up as much of that volume as possible.

The goal of your business is to capture as many customer shopping dollars as possible. And you have the KIT to do it.

The reason KIT works is that your customers want to hear from you. They shop your business. They spend their money with you. They trust you. Your letter in the mail or your voice over the phone is familiar, comfortable, easy. People do things from habit.

Of course, there are the adventurers who want to vacation in a different city every year. But there are far more who buy the second home or condominium in a familiar place because they are "comfortable" there. People are uncomfortable in a new place or strange surroundings. Doctors tell us when patients wake up from an operation they do not say, "Who am I?" they say, "Where am I?" Everyone wants to be familiar, comfortable, at home.

And your customers feel that way in your place of business. If something happens with your business and they are not informed, they are resentful. It's like a friend telling secrets and leaving you out. You get mad. That is what happened to Roger Bailey, a bank officer in Grand Island, Nebraska.

He wrote us: "We sent an extensive mailing to customers advertising our ATMs (Automatic Teller Machines). One was inadvertently sent empty — the addressed envelope but nothing inside. The customer called and asked what was in the envelope. After all, if it came from her bank, it must be important.

"I apologized, explained the brochure and thought that ended the conversation. I was wrong. The customer insisted I send the brochure anyway. She wanted to see what she missed from her bank . . . "

What all this proves is that your customers care. They want to know. They will respond to your calling or writing, your KIT.

And so when business is off and sales are down and you stare at the front doors wondering when the next customer will come in, start planning on what you will do today to let your present customers know you are there to cherish, love, and fall over them.

They're your list! And you can pack up your troubles in your old KIT bag and smile, smile, smile.

TYPES OF LISTS

Prospect List

Your best list is a list of current customers. Your next best list is your prospect list. What's a *prospect?* A prospect is someone who has shown an interest in your products or services but who has not yet bought (he or she may be a *customer* for one item but a *prospect* for another.)

Rented List

A list broker once told me if I needed a list of left-handed golfers he could get it for me.

First thought: "Wow!"

Second thought: It probably isn't too difficult. Find a manufacturer of custom golf clubs and rent his customer list of lefties.

That's how it is with lists. They're available for almost any specific kind of prospective buyer. You name the audience and there's a list. (It's been estimated that there are over 50,000 lists.)

Where do these lists come from?

People who have customer lists often rent them either directly to you or through list brokers.

Where do you find the people who rent these lists?

First stop: the classified section of your telephone directory under the heading "Mailing Lists." Here you'll find not only sources for national lists but also sources for local lists and names of firms who will help you maintain your own lists.

Next ... get a copy from the library (or buy a copy) of *Standard Rate & Data Service* (SRDS) *Guide to Consumer Mailing Lists* (3004 Glenview Road, Wilmette, IL 60091. Phone: 1-800-323-4601.) This book has pages and pages of listings of almost all available lists with detailed information about each list.

Borrowed Lists

Trade publications sometimes let their advertisers borrow their subscribers list. They won't actually *give you* the names for you to use but will ask you to furnish *them* with *your* mailing.

They will address and mail, charging you for the postage. People are *very* fussy about who actually sees their list.

You might also try swapping lists with a friendly business that does not have competitive products or services. We have helped several clients by putting them together for list swaps.

Compiled Lists

These are lists of names and addresses of people or firms without respect to whether or not they ever bought anything by mail. Typically they could be lists from local or state governments, lists from directories, or automobile owners lists (in states where their sale is still legal).

The Different Ways to Maintain Your Mailing List (Advantage/ Disadvantage)

3" x 5" cards
　　For up to about 500 names.
　　Inexpensive.
　　Easy to check for duplicate names or addresses.
But ...
　　Each name has to be typed each time.
　　Best for first class mailings.

Computer
　　For about 3,000 to 5,000 names or more.
　　Inexpensive to add names.
　　Easy to check on duplicates.
　　Computer can also write letters, keep track of accounts.
　　Can rearrange names for zip coding.

But ...

There is an initial investment in equipment.

Requires good planning.

You have to back up your data.

Mailing House

Work done by someone else. Doesn't disturb your routine.

Mailing goes from printer to post office.

But ...

Costs more.

You don't have the tight control over your mailer.

Sometimes you have to wait for your mailings until they take care of a bigger customer.

TOOLBOX

Compute your profits

PROBABLY THE MOST significant change in direct mail in recent years has been the computer — particularly the inexpensive personal computer.

Now it's possible for the smallest direct mailer to maintain his own list with the ability to print addresses or labels.

The computer, with appropriate software, can be used as a word processor to write copy, or to personalize letters, or to file and store test results for mailings. Like its many other applications, the computer has dramatically changed our ability to produce more effective direct mail. If your business already has a computer, you may be able to adapt the equipment you use for other purposes and use that equipment to help you produce direct mail.

For many, the big problem is the selection of appropriate equipment and software. What should you buy? How much should you spend? Veterans of this selection process advise that the software decision should come before the hardware decision.

Ask yourself: What do you want your computer to do?

A careful analysis must be made to determine what you want to accomplish:

- How much information do you want to store?
- In how many varied forms?
- How fast do you need to retrieve this information?
- How many people need access to the equipment?
- And when?
- What about budget?

These are all questions to answer *before you* make the decision for both software and hardware

Considering the tremendous variety of equipment and programs available, the best help on what to buy is from other business friends who use computers for direct mail. Start with your local computer store and ask them to recommend equipment and software give you references of other business people who have used their services.

If you cannot get adequate help from a reputable dealer, try a consultant. The small consulting fee will save you large financial mistakes.

Let's look at some effective uses of the computer for your direct mail program.

Mailing Lists

Your best customers are your current customers. With the computer you can maintain a mailing list of customers each time you produce an order or write a quotation or send a bill.

You can also build a list of prospects by adding names picked up from other sources.

The computer, with the right software, allows you to *segment* your mailing list. Example: You are a manufacturer of electronic parts. You can code and recall purchasing names, engineering names and management names. Retailers might code on a "last time bought" basis and call up those names of people who have not made recent purchases. A video store might segment according to a viewer's *tastes.*

Best of all, segmentation is not limited to one function. You can build in multiple variables to further refine your audience.

Addressing

Having selected the names you want to use, your computer is now ready for addressing. You have the option of address labels or of individually addressing letters and envelopes from the names stored in memory.

Customers and businesses are familiar with mailing labels. Label addressing is almost always as effective as typewritten. For smaller, highly personalized letters (remember direct mail is a *personal* medium), you can enter individual names into stock letters stored in the memory of a computer.

Important: Yes, your computer can "drop" the person's name throughout the letter and it becomes a high form of personalization.

Caution: Tests have shown that many readers *resent* too much personalization. You've seen those letters. The ones that tell you what street you live on, the make of your car and the school your child goes to every day. This is a turn-off to many customers. They feel Orwell and Big Brother have arrived in the morning mail.

And the most personal letter is the least personal letter if the name is misspelled. The daily mail is filled with letters and packages to Endman, Herdman, Erman, Ratfeld, Rapehel, Rafel and more . . . If you begin your "personal" letter with "Dear Erdman, Kenneth B.," we never make it to the opening sentence.

Word Processing

If you are writing your copy in house, the word processing capabilities of your computer are invaluable for both time savings and accuracy. The ability to constantly review and make changes on the screen before printing is a definite aid to creativity.

Testing

The computer offers a convenient way to store test information for future recall as the least of its test functions. Beyond that, when you get involved in more sophisticated testing, the computer will be the tool to solve mathematical problems and produce the statistical results you'll need.

When you put information on a computer, remember the formula: Garbage In, Garbage Out. What that means: If you put the wrong information into the computer, you will receive wrong information back. This is important when you spell names, enter addresses. But it is vital when you are putting in the zip code. A misplaced, forgotten or transposed number simply makes your mailing piece ineffective because it just doesn't get there . . .

In his introduction to Murray's book, *But Would Saks Fifth Avenue Do It?,* publisher Pete Hoke of *Direct Marketing* magazine tells the story of Kermit Goldberg from Baltimore.

"One of Kermit's constant concerns over the years was the logic of huge sale ads in newspapers. Wasn't this a public announcement that the merchant had bought too much, or the wrong merchandise? Didn't sale advertising make some customers wonder why they should buy at regular prices? Did the sale really move the merchandise out?

Kermit woke up one night with a great idea. What if, he mused, I put the suit size of every sale on my new computer? He did so the next day. In a year, he had his answer. Experience had shown that if he had ten 43 longs left after the season, he would need to select only the customers off the file who had bought 43 longs. A simple computer message sent to this small list, inviting each individual to come into the store the following week to buy another suit in their size at 20 percent off, would sell the ten suits. At a cost of about $7. And no city-wide announcement of Clearance, Clearance, Clearance at full page newspaper rates.

Is that direct mail? Sure. Highly selective? Of course! And just one application of the medium.

Remember, it may look like a computer, but when properly used it will work like a cash register ringing up those extra sales.

The two major uses of computers for small businesses doing direct mail are (1) mailing list storage, and (2) word processing. Those functions consist of . . .

Correcting, editing, updating: You can make corrections as you are typing. You can store all the information and bring it up on the computer screen at a future date adding, subtracting, changing the information you have stored.

Selecting. You can bring up certain names and addresses without going through the entire list (see examples that follow).

Calculating. You have a built in math department that adds, subtracts, multiplies, divides for you.

Storing. You have all the information you want or need on a paper thin *disc* instead of books, papers and bulky files.

Merging: You have some new, up-to-date information. This can be *merged* into the material you already have.

Computers may not be for you if:

• Used rarely. You decide to begin. You will send a notice of your twice-a-year sale. And maybe some kind of announcement in between. Start small. Do not use a computer.

• Small list. Your mailing list is a couple of hundred names. Keep the names on 3" x 5" cards. Or have them typed on address labels with three carbons by a local secretarial service. *Do not use a computer.*

Computers are not for everybody. But many businesses can profit from the speed and reliability of today's relatively inexpensive computer.

5

I'm Going to Make You
an Offer You Can't Refuse

"WERE GOING TO PLAY a fun game tonight," said the hostess as the guests arrived.

After dinner she explained the game.

Each person would have someone's name taped to his or her back. They would then ask anyone in the room questions about this "person." Each had ten minutes to guess the name of their mystery person.

The famous ones were easy. The movie stars took only a few minutes. But half-way through the evening, one person simply could not guess the name on his back. He asked all the right questions and finally, at the ten minute limit, gave up.

"Don't you really have any idea who the person could be?" asked the hostess.

"No," he replied. "None of the descriptions or answers seemed in the least bit familiar."

The hostess took off the name and showed it to him.

It was his own.

What happened?

This: Each of us has an image of who we are to ourselves that does not necessarily correspond to who we are to others.

This point of view is very important to remember in direct mail. For if we are marketing directly to an individual (and we are), we must understand their point of view *before* we write any words.

Remember, every one of your potential customers is listening to an

FM radio station in his home. The call letters are WII-FM.

This station has a clear channel and broadcasts across the entire world. Your customers listen to this station twenty-four hours a day. Consciously while they are awake. Subconsciously while they are sleeping. Your job, as an advertiser, is to put your commercial on this station.

Oh, by the way, the initials WII-FM stand for What's In It For Me?

The customer knows what's in it for you. He spends *his* money in *your* place of business. But . . . what's in it for *him?* Why should he shop with you or buy your services instead of your competition's? What are you doing to make your offer more attractive, unusual . . . profitable?

To answer that question, you have to know there is really one basic rule to success in selling. Here it is. Just memorize this one sentence, follow what it says and your success is assured: FIND OUT WHAT YOUR CUSTOMERS WANT AND GIVE IT TO THEM.

Now reprint that phrase and put it on the wall in front of your desk where you can read it before you start your next direct mail campaign.

What we are *not* talking about in this chapter is what you have to sell. We are *not* talking about your bank's Certificate of Deposit, your store's clothing, your professional service, your new, just-arrived item in the warehouse.

Those are products or services.

What we *are* talking about is how to sell those products or services

That's what we mean by offer. What do you *offer* the customer so he *wants* to buy? Your offer is the way you present your product or service, the benefits and the price in terms of the reader's desires, needs, wants, dreams. Now, your offer has to be what the customer wants to buy. Not what you think she wants to buy.

How do you find out?

Remember the fellow at the party who didn't know it was his name on his back? Try that for starters. What is your customer's point of view? What are the **benefits** she will receive?

Some tire salesmen feel they should tell customers how steel belted tires are made with seven cords of steel wrapped together to form strong reinforcement. But we want to hear how safe the tires are when our spouse drives the children to school.

Travel agents do not sell the time payments needed to buy the airline tickets. They sell romance, glamour, excitement.

Clothing salesmen do not sell stitches to the inch. They sell fashion, style, appeal to the opposite sex.

We all know businesspeople who say, "I'm going to buy what I like for my store. If the customer doesn't like it, too bad."

Well, too bad for those businesspeople. They soon fold up their retailing tent and wonder where they went wrong.

This does not mean your individual taste and selection and choice does not enter into what you sell. Of course it does.

What it does mean: After establishing certain parameters, guidelines and choices, how do you find out what your customer wants to buy? People's taste and style and choice of what they want to eat, wear, watch, read or participate in continually changes. In some cases gradually. In some, overnight.

Somewhere in this promised land there are warehouses full of men's Nehru shirts and women's satin hot pants and hula hoops and blotters waiting for that style to return. Someday. Maybe. Great ideas whose time came . . . and went. We can be sure the only thing that remains constant . . . is change.

As a business person, how do you know, really *know,* what product or service your customer wants to buy?

When you have a new product or service, instead of sending out your next mailing piece to your entire mailing list, why not simply "test" it with a percentage of your mailing list? A very, very small percentage of your list will show you what the probable results would be if you mail the entire list. (More on testing in Chapter 15).

Testing is extremely valuable to you if you really believe in your product and feel it offers a benefit to your customer. Your first mailing may not be profitable. This does not necessarily mean the offer you made is bad. It may mean the *approach you* made is not working. People who use direct mail and claim they are merely advertising products to fill their customer's "needs" are living in the wrong century. We have not been a "needy" country for more than fifty years. Today's successful businesses are not need-fillers. They are want-creators.

As little children we are asked by adults, "What do you want to be when you grow up?" No one says, "What do you *need* to be?"

The reason is simple. If you "want" something strongly enough, you will produce it, work for it or buy it.

Our job, as salespeople, is to create *wants*. One way we can do this is by listening to our customers. All of us in selling are usually so concerned with getting across a message of what we want to sell we don't take the time to listen to what the customer wants to buy.

Your customers care. They will respond to your calling or writing as long as you can make an offer to them of something they want.

THE PSYCHOLOGY OF THE SECOND INTEREST

Making a sale is simply finding out what the customer wants to buy and giving it to her. At this point you might well ask, "What if what I have to sell is not what *they* want to buy?"

Good question. And time to try a selling technique we call, "The Psychology of the Second Interest." Here's what it means:

You can have someone buy something you want to sell them if you offer them something else they want to buy.

Here's an example: Do children buy Crackerjacks for the carmel popcorn . . . or the prize?

Do you buy a new fragrance for the fragrance or for the free umbrella or low cost baggage that is yours with every purchase? Do you subscribe to magazines for the magazine or the chance to win $100,000 a year for life? Or a new home? Or a new car?

Do you go to conventions to go to conventions or because it's a tax deductible reason to visit San Francisco?

Take a look at breakfast cereal boxes in your kitchen cabinet. Post Grape Nuts offered a chance to win "free athletic equipment for your school" by saving the seals on the side of the cereal box. Del Monte raisins offered you an embossed hardcover world atlas (300 pages, 190 in full color) for half price if you sent in the label.

Next time you try selling what you want to sell, what **additional** offer can you make that the customer wants to buy?

GIVE YOUR CUSTOMERS A CHOICE

Customers like a choices. The more ways you offer your customer to buy from you in the mail, the greater your response.

Ways to pay. If the product must be bought with cash, you eliminate a lot of buyers. Each new way you give them to purchase your product, you increase sales: Credit cards. C.O.D.'s, time payments, 30-day charges, checks . . .

Special price offers. The item can be bought for a reduced price but only for a specified length of time. Give the exact date and hold to it.

Discount for quantity. If you buy now, the price is so much less. And if you buy five it's even less.

Free information. Even if they do *not* buy the product, have them respond to some brochure, booklet, newsletter, something you give them free for simply checking the appropriate box.

Free gift. You've all seen this one. If you order the item, you also receive, free of charge, this special . . . something. And you keep the something whether or not you decide to keep the item ordered. (A free gift can increase your orders by at least 25 percent!) But select a gift suited to *personal* use. It will have far more appeal.

Not if but which. Always give your customer a choice between something and something, not something and nothing. We succeed in selling clothing because we always ask the customer to make a decision *between* items, never a yes/no decision:

"Do you like white or pastel shirts?"

"Do you like striped or solid ties?"

"Do you like button down or plain collar shirts?" Make the same offer in your mailing. Give the customer a choice. Ask them *which* they prefer.

TOOLBOX
The Guarantee

In 1861, the Austrian foreign minister, Johann Berhnard Graf Von Rechberg was asked to comment upon papers recently drawn with guarantees concerning the recognition of Italy. His comment, "Guarantees are not worth the paper they are written on."

True in 1861. Not true today. Especially with the Federal Trade Commission watching.

Guarantees inspire confidence. Nearly 100 years ago, Sears Roebuck guaranteed satisfaction for everything in their catalogue. Nearly half a century ago *Good Housekeeping* made the word famous with their "satisfaction guaranteed or replacement of merchandise."

THROUGH THE YEARS, NO ONE HAS SUCCEEDED IN MAIL ORDER WITHOUT OFFERING THE CONSUMER A GUARANTEE.

Norm Thompson in Portland, Oregon copyrighted their "You be the Judge" guarantee. They guarantee their merchandise for the normal life of the product, "you being the judge of what that normal life should be."

Publix supermarkets in Florida advertise their food is guaranteed until you have enjoyed every morsel. When the senior citizens were asked why they shopped Publix some answered, "Because they guarantee their food." It was pointed out to them all supermarkets guarantee their food. "Really?" said the skeptical ones, "how come they don't say so?" (Which is one reason why Publix owns 25% of every food dollar spent in Florida.)

Guarantee your merchandise you sell! Do not assume your customer knows you do. Tell them. *And don't make exceptions.*

Make it simple to read and understand. L.L. Bean in Maine simply says, "Our products are guaranteed to be 100% satisfactory. Return anything purchased from us that proves otherwise. We will replace it or refund your money as you wish." (See the full L.L. Bean guarantee on the next page)

Any teacher or good student of direct mail will tell you how important a guarantee is when selling your merchandise through the mail. It gives you an added advantage because the customer now has confidence he can trust you.

If a customer brought defective merchandise back to you or was even simply dissatisfied with your product would you try to make the customer happy? Would you offer a refund or a replacement of money? If you wanted to see that customer again, you would. That is why the overwhelming number of catalogs and products sold through the mail highlight their guarantee. They want to *make sure* their customer is satisfied.

Well, with one notable exception: many department stores. Those established institutions of retailing throughout the country send many pieces through the mail offering goods and services for sale. But rarely do they offer the same guarantee printed in the catalogue that you find from a competitive company doing most of their business through the mail and often times selling the exact same product as the department store.

Why do so many stores and businesses leave out the guarantee in their mailings even though, in reality they do "guarantee" what they sell?

Here's what some answered: "Those catalogs go to our customers. They know who we are. They know we will guarantee everything we sell."

Do they?

And aren't the other folks sending out catalogues sending them to *their* customers? And yet they repeat the guarantee in every issue.

Do you think someone should tell some of those that take the customer for granted about the Curse of Assumption?

L. L. Bean Guarantee

It began with a waterproof shoe to go duck hunting. And now this Maine retailer does more than $250 million a year selling merchandise through the mail. And his guarantee has not changed through the years because . . . it works.

100% GUARANTEE

All of our products are guaranteed to give 100% satisfaction in every way. Return anything purchased from us at any time if it proves otherwise. We will replace it, refund your purchase price or credit your credit card, as you wish. We do not want you to have anything from L.L. Bean that is not completely satisfactory.

Eddie Bauer Guarantee

Known originally for selling warm jackets, this mail marketeer is known for his quality merchandise and his very, very simple guarantee that literally tells you like it is.

OUR GUARANTEE

**Every item we sell will give
complete satisfaction or you may
return it for a full refund.**

The Sharper Image Guarantee

Clearly spelled out to (1) give you thirty days to make up your mind (2) say their price is the lowest and (3) have a one-year quality guarantee.

THREE REASONS WHY YOU ENJOY SHOPPING MORE WITH **THE SHARPER IMAGE**.

1. You have 30 days to make up your mind.

If not satisfied, simply return the item (in new condition, please) within 30 days for a prompt, courteous refund, whatever the reason. Your satisfaction is the only judge.

2. You get the best value. We match any advertised price.

You won't see the same item advertised for less elsewhere. If you do; just send us the advertisement within 30 days of receiving the item. We'll refund or credit the difference to you.

3. You own a durable, well-made product, with a one-year quality guarantee.

We make sure every product is backed by a reputable manufacturer's service center. If you don't get prompt satisfactory service, in or out of warranty, call our Customer Relations representatives. Use the toll free Customer Relations number 800-344-5555. We'll make sure your item is fixed or replaced in a reasonable time, or your money will be refunded — up to a full year after purchase.

Norm Thompson Guarantee

This is our favorite. Not only because they have *trademarked* their guarantee but also because they spell it out in very explicit terms telling you it is *not* a 2-week guarantee but good for the normal life of the product and the clincher line, You being the judge of what the normal life should be . . .

"You be the Judge™" Guarantee

When we say You be the Judge™, we mean just that! Every product you purchase from Norm Thompson must live up to YOUR expectations, not ours. If at any time a product fails to satisfy you, return it to us, postage prepaid, and we will either replace the item, or refund your money In full, whichever you wish.

This is definitely not a 2-week guarantee. Its good for the normal life of the product. (You being the judge of what that normal life should be.) We'll stand behind everything we sell to the fullest extent...no ifs, ands or buts.

PART TWO

PRODUCING YOUR MAILER

When I was young I observed that nine out of every ten things I did were failures, so I did ten times more work.
— **George Bernard Shaw**

6

OFF WITH THEIR HEADS!

SEVEN OUT OF ten people will read the headline on your direct mailer. But only three out of ten will keep on reading.

The headline is a most important part of your direct mail piece because it is at this point the reader decides whether or not they will continue reading from the top of your mailer to the copy that follows.

Your headline should have one of two appeals (best of all, both).

1. The headline should *promise a benefit.*
2. The headline should *provoke curiosity.*

David Ogilvy, founder of Ogilvy and Mather, one of the world's greatest advertising agencies, tells of the time he gathered his new copywriters into a room and said, "Ladies and gentlemen, when you have written the headline for your ad, you have spent 75 percent of your client's money."

What was he saying? This: unless you capture the readers' attention up front and hold their interest, you will not create a desire to buy.

Readership surveys show that the average person will spend about four seconds on a newspaper page. One, two, three, four, turn the page. And in those four seconds the readers will glance at the headlines on the news columns *before* they look at the headlines on the ads, yours included. Unless your headline promises a benefit or provokes curiosity they will miss your message.

You can have the most fascinating, interesting, makes-me-want-to-buy copy in your ad. But if the headline does not stop me and keep me reading, that great copy will never be read.

Remember: In an average newspaper, your headline competes for attention with about 300 *other* headlines.

Bill Jayme, one of America's best direct mail advertising writers, once told us he spends about one-third of his time just thinking about the headline. The rest of the time goes into the multi-page hundreds of words that follows. His theory: It doesn't do any good to write the best copy in the world if no one bothers to read past the headline. (Asked to come up with an attention-grabbing headline for the **outside** of an envelope carrying subscription letters for a new restaurant magazine, Jayme wrote: "How much should you tip when you're planning to pocket the ashtray?")

John Caples, Vice President of BBD, a member of the Advertising Hall of Fame who is now deceased, once put together a series of different headlines for the same product, a retirement insurance plan from Phoenix Mutual. He found to his amazement that by simply changing the headline, he could double, triple, and in one test, receive *twenty times* the response of the original headline . . . just by using a new (and obviously more effective) headline.

Think of your headline as a good salesman in your business. Headlines command attention by offering the customer a reason to buy. The best ads and direct mailers are the ones that sell, not necessarily the ones that win awards.

John Kennedy, one of the greatest advertising copywriters in advertising history, applied for his first job by sending a note to Albert Lasker, president of the Lord & Thomas advertising agency, saying, "I have the best definition for advertising you have ever seen."

Intrigued, the agency head invited him to his office and asked what it was. Kennedy answered, "Advertising is salesmanship in print."

He got the job.

What that means: A good ad is one that sells. And selling begins with first impressions.

The headline on the envelope of your mailer competes with the other direct mail envelopes in the mailbox. This means you must know the techniques that work in the writing of the headline on the outside of your envelope or the beginning of your letter.

Here are ten ways to develop good headline *have-its:*

1. *Have it* appeal to self-interest.
2. Have it arouse curiosity.
3. Have it for the right audience.
4. Have it easy to understand.
5. Have it newsworthy.
6. Have it believable.
7. Have it produce quick results.
8. Have it specific.
9. Have it something of value.
10. Have it well-known.

Let's take them one at a time and see how they work.

1. Have it appeal to self-interest. What benefit does the headline offer me? The best-selling headline of all times, *How to Win Friends and Influence People,* the title of Dale Carnegie's book, was the third title tried. And it has resulted in one of the best sellers of all times. Because *everyone* wants to have friends. And influence people. Here are some other headlines that work:

"How to make a million dollars in mail order."

"How to lose 10 pounds in 10 days."

"How to retire on $25,000 a year."

"Are you spending $10 a week too much for food?"

2. Have it arouse curiosity. Stop your reader with a statement that makes him ask, "How can *that* be?" And/or, "What do they mean by that?" And/or, "Does that mean what I think it means?"

Examples . . .

"Do you wonder how we can sell an all-wool shetland sweater for less than $15?"

"How to look younger in 14 days."

"How many of these 20 questions can you answer correctly?"

The last example follows a basic direct mail guideline: get the customer involved.

As soon as you have the customer not only reading but also have them acting ("Peel off this label" . . . "Fill in this coupon" . . . "Cut along this line") then your results will increase dramatically.

Important: You must answer the question you raise in the headline in the copy that follows. And the answer must make logical sense. *Because* you are having a sale. *Because* you made a special purchase. *Because* you are offering your customers a pre-season chance to buy before you advertise to the world. The customers' curiosity must be satisfied by your explanation. Otherwise they simply will not respond now and, more importantly, they will view any future mailings from you skeptically. A shocking statistic: 90 percent of Americans do *not* associate the word "trust" with the word "business."

And "trust" is a key word in direct mail. Always remember direct mail's *greatest* strength is the personal relationship between you and your customer. If you arouse your customer's curiosity in the headline, answer it logically and sensibly in the copy that follows to keep that trust.

3. Have it for the right audience. Never forget the two most important ingredients in a successful direct mail package are (a) the list and (b) the offer.

The List. You start off with a giant advantage, your list. Your own customers. People who trust and believe in you because they have invested their money with you in the past. They know you.

The professionals call these names a "database." Don't be confused by this term. It means the list of your customer's names.

Your customers are obviously your right audience. When looking to expand your mailing list and using new lists, make sure these new names are as close as possible to your present customers in terms of age/salary/ location/lifestyle.

Professionals use words like geographics, demographics, psychographics. They are simply another way of saying to make sure your names are similar to your present customers in terms of age/salary/where they live . . . etc.

The offer. Only suggest or recommend a product the customer wants. Start with what customers are presently buying from you.

If a customer is near retirement you do not offer the same package you would to a newlywed. Or grass seed to apartment dwellers. Some of the direct mail experts say the best mailer is only 20 percent devoted to creativity. The other 80 percent is divided equally between the right product or service . . . and the right list.

4. Have it easy to understand. Most of us talk in two languages, one when we are talking to one another, the second when we sit down to write something. We suddenly become a different person, very erudite and much more difficult to understand. When writing a headline (or copy) make it easy to understand. Do *not* use words peculiar to your specific kind of business. Each industry has a jargon that only insiders know. What will work in a trade magazine will not work in a general publication or a wide spread direct mail campaign.

And do *not* talk in terms of the *features* of the product. But talk in terms of *benefits*. Forget the detailed analysis. Say what the item will do for the reader.

If a jacket is down-filled say, "Twice the warmth at half the weight."

If an insurance policy has lower rates for non-smokers say, "Double the coverage for the same premium."

If the tires are steel belted, say, "When you're away from home, your family is riding on the safest tires ever designed."

A recent bank headline said, "Every officer in our establishment receives a thrill whenever a loan is consummated."

Who talks like that?

Now, if the headline said, "Here's the money you need to open your shop" . . . well, everyone understands *that*.

5. Have it newsworthy. Look at the direct mail pieces you receive in the mail. Notice how many times you see these words in headlines: *New. Announcing. For the first time. Introducing. Free.*

There's a reason. They work.

Cereals and soups are constantly promoted as "New and improved." So are toothpaste, soap and gasoline.

If you can tie in a recent news story with your product, that works well. If the paper runs a story about your business, clip it out and reprint it as a mailer for prospective customers with the headline, "Did you see this story in the paper?"

Customers respond favorably to that which is new, the latest, just out. Everyone wants to be at the front of the line when the store opens.

Some writers say a headline is like a billboard. Once you have more than six or eight words, it is not read. Not true.

New York University's School of Retailing ran headline tests working with a large department store. Their conclusion: headlines with ten words *or more* sold more than short headlines.

The trick: The words must contain *news or information.*

6. *Have it believable.* The headline that begins, "This is your last chance to . . ." is the one I never finish reading. I know a similar (or better) offer will follow in the next mail.

The mailer with the headline that says, "How to make a million dollars in your spare time" quickly finds its way to the nearest wastepaper basket.

A recent advertisement for light bulbs showed the top of a light bulb broken off with the headline, "Don't bite off more than you can chew." I was tempted to write them and tell them I bit off only as much as shown in the picture and now I had this pain in my stomach and my attorney said . . .

An ad for truck sales showed a truck in the middle of a sesame seed bun with the headline, "More than one million sold." A take off on the McDonald's theme but I really do not want to buy a truck that fits inside a sesame seed bun.

We agree with David Ogilvy's line, "The customer is not a moron. She's your wife."

Writers who look for the cute (and irrelevant) phrase, the clever pun, the gimmick angle wind up with headlines that are often looked at . . . but not believed.

If you offer a well-known product at too low a price, the customer asks, "What's the gimmick? It simply doesn't make sense." It is not believable. And therefore it's ignored. Tossed away.

7. Have it produce quick results. Americans are accustomed to speed. The success of the newspaper USA *Today is* because the format closely parallels the nightly TV news. A condensation of what happened that day without too much detail. Everything complete on one page. And preferably in one or two paragraphs.

If you can show how someone can lose weight quickly, make money quickly, be successful in a short period of time in a believable manner, people will read what you have to say.

8. Have it specific. What does "Half-price sale" mean? Yes, it means one half the original price. But if you do not list the original price . . . what does "half-price sale" mean? Half of what?

When banks offer savings in terms of percentages . . . what do the percentages mean? If they would offer the return in dollars . . . well, that we understand.

A Texas bank did just that. Did people really "understand" the numbers game the banks was playing in its ads? That was the question asked by Doug McDougal, marketing officer of Victoria National Bank in Victoria, Texas. His competitive market included four banks, three savings and loans within a 60,000 population.

The problem: His bank was the last to advertise money market certificates. When they finally decided to do it, they were faced with the problem of what to do differently from the competition?

They examined all the ads and they noticed that all the competition advertised percentages. No one advertised *dollars.*

This was their 11-word headline: "Deposit $10,000 today. Walk out with $10,476 in only six months."

McDougal's advertising budget was $1,450. This gave the bank two newspaper ads every week for seven weeks. Here's what happened, in Doug's words: "We had been taking in $70,000 daily in new money market certificates before the ad broke. That figure jumped immediately to *$250,000* daily. One day we sold $521,000. Many customers came in with the ad in their hand."

In one year the bank took in more than four *million* dollars in new money for money market certificates.

Not bad for an investment of $1,450. And simply because they talked in specific terms of dollars rather than percentages.

Barney's clothing store in New York City has been running twice-a year sales with the headline, "100 Reasons to Shop Barney's Summer Sale" or "100 Reasons to Shop Barney's Winter Sale."

They list 100 items they have on sale. The customers keep on reading and reading and reading . . . and then buying and buying and buying.

People have a strange attraction to numbers. From the Ten Commandments to the "Seven out of ten people who..." to "The 19 reasons why" to the "16 people who believe that...," not only do people read the headline and then start reading the copy . . . but more amazingly, they have to read down to the last number mentioned.

The more specific you are in your headline, the more selective you are in targeting your audience.

"An important message to men who are losing their hair . . ." "How college students can earn their tuition this summer."

9. *Have it something of value.* The cosmetics people have this down to an exact science. They call it "purchase with purchase." If you buy one of their products, you receive a gift for free or for a fraction of its true value.

Offer benefits you have that make you separate and different from and put you in front of the competition: free parking, free gift wrapping, free delivery, free monogramming . . .

- Make it a collectible. ("If you bought this anniversary plate five years ago for $10, you could sell it for $50 today.")
- Make it priceworthy. ("Would you buy this $75 designer blouse for $29?")
- Make it within a time limit ("After June 1st, this computer will sell for $500. Now it is yours for $350")
- Make it fulfill a dream ("To men who want to quit work some day.")
- Make it address a weakness ("How I improved my memory in one evening.")
- Make it eliminate a drudgery ("How to prepare a complete and delicious meal in only 60 minutes.")

10. Have it well known. David Ogilvy said, "Include the brand name in the headline." A good idea. Whenever possible. But putting in the name just for putting in the name is not good enough.

If your name has a reason for being there, fine. Because you are the first to . . . because you are the place where . . . because you are known for . . . all good reasons. But simply putting your store's name in *without a reason* may make you feel good but will not do a thing for your customer.

Brand names are important because they make the reader feel comfortable. Readers know about a specific brand and will respond in a more positive manner than to an unfamiliar brand.

Using testimonials fills the same well known need. Customers react positively to endorsements by well-known people. Otherwise why are all these advertising agencies paying all that money? Many sport celebrities earn much more on the testimonial circuit than on the playing field. The reason why: They are well known.

TOOLBOX

A BAKER'S DOZEN
OF HEADLINE WORDS

Now that you know the reasons why headlines work, are there certain words that seem to work in headlines better than other words?

Yes.

The following words are seen in the most successful headlines. They trigger positive emotional responses from your customers. Try one (or more) of this baker's dozen of headlines words next time you are writing the headline for your next direct mailer:

1. *Free.* Still number one. Everyone wants to know what they can have at no cost.
2. *New.* Everyone wants to have what is "in," be the first on the block with the latest car, dress, hairdo, latest technology. Great word (well, unless you're selling antiques).
3. *Now.* Gives a sense of immediacy. Quick. Hurry. Don't be late.
4. *Wanted.* What's wanted? By whom? For how much? Where?
5. *Announcing.* Something just happened and you're the first to know.
6. *How.* Most often seen as *"How to . . ."* and followed by a strong benefit.
7. *Win.* Which accounts for the tremendous success of sweepstakes, bingo parlors, Las Vegas and Atlantic City.
8. *Guarantee.* We all want to be reassured. There is no risk if I buy from you. Tell me how long you have been in business. Make the guarantee big, bold, prominent (near the order blank if you are asking for an order) and *simple.*

9. *Easy.* *If* what you have to sell takes less effort to do a job I am presently doing, say so. (Or by making it easy for the reader to buy your product.)
10. *You.* People are interested in themselves. The more you use "you" in your headlines the more you will increase your readership. (That's five times in just one sentence.)
11. *Save.* Everyone wants to save something, somewhere, sometime.
12. *At last.* From the song of the same name. Has the feel of something that has happened that you always wanted to happen.
13. *Breakthrough.* Joe Sugarman, one of the country's top copywriters, says every time he uses the word "breakthrough" in his headlines, his sales increase. He used "Printer Breakthrough" for ten years in his catalogs for the same calculator, and it worked every time. Other businesses have copied Sugarman's magic word with excellent results.

7

TAKE OUR WORD FOR IT

"When I use a word," Humpty Dumpty said in rather a scornful tone, "it means just what I choose it to mean neither more nor less."

"The question is," said Alice, "whether you can make the words mean so many different things."

"The question is," said Humpty Dumpty, "which is to be master — that's all."

--Alice in Wonderland

Copy: The Long & Short of It

How long should your copy be?

There is the short school and the long school of copy writers.

The short school includes the ones who insist all memos must be on one page. Preferably double spaced.

The long school says to write all the information you have in your mailing.

The correct answer is to write until you finish what you want to say. People will keep on reading as long as it is interesting for them to keep on reading.

In a recent interview, David Ogilvy summed up the advantage of using long copy in direct marketing. "Experience has taught us that short copy doesn't sell . . . We pack our advertisements and letters with information about the product. We have have found out we have to — if we want to sell anything."

We would hesitate to argue with David Ogilvy, one of the premier advertising practitioners of all time. And our bias is for long copy.

But occasionally, short copy can pack a wallop. Our favorite long *vs.* short copy story concerns the landlord who decided to evict his tenants. His lawyer sent all the residents a thick, legal long-copy document listing all the reasons they had to move.

One tenant responded with this classic short-style copy:

Dear Sir,
I remain
Very truly yours.

Every one of your mailing pieces is a complete sales pitch for your product. Sometimes you can say it all in five words. Sometimes it takes five hundred.

But as long as it is interesting to read, the reader will read.

Many studies show readership falls off quickly up to the first 50 words. But if they read the first 50, they will probably read the next 500.

Boyce Morgan, the writer responsible for many of the early direct mail successes of the *Kiplinger Letter* once conducted tests on long vs. short copy. His results: when you cut copy down to simply fit on *one* sheet of paper you also cut down on orders.

The "more you tell, the more you sell" school of writing is championed by Dr. Charles Edwards of the Graduate School of Retailing at New York University. He says, "The more facts you tell, the more you sell. An advertisement's chance for success increases as the number of pertinent merchandise facts indicated in the advertisement increases."

Famous advertising writer Claude Hopkins once wrote five pages of copy to promote Schlitz beer. Schlitz's sales moved from fifth place to first place in a short time.

Writer Vic Schwab tells the story of Max Hart (of Hart, Schaffner & Marx). Hart disliked long copy. He continually rejected ads with too many words. One day his advertising manager said, "I'll bet you ten dollars I can write a newspaper ad of just copy and you will read every word. And you will agree if I just show you just the headline."

Hart took the bet, read the headline and said, "OK, you win. Run the ad."

This was the headline: "This ad is all about Max Hart."

DOES YOUR WRITING SOUND LIKE YOU TALKING?

Every expert you talk to on direct mail will tell you to "write as you talk." Which is fine. Up to a point.

If you tape recorded how you sold your product to a customer you would be amazed at how many "Uhhhs" and "ahhhs" and those unforgivable "I," "me" and "ours" that fill out your selling talk.

Yes, of course, it is admirable, effective and to be desired to "write as you talk." But your writing should be *edited*. Your conversation is chock-full of many useless words that do not add a single selling point to your effective letter or mailer.

Conversation is also connected with body language that is difficult if not impossible eto put into your writing. How do you define a twitch of your eye, a shrug of your shoulder, an expressive gesture with your hands each accompanied by a related phrase.

What "write as you talk" *really* means is that the copy should be smooth and easy to read as good conversation is easy to hear.

Marketing consultant Andrew Byrne, says there are only three deadly failures in advertising:

1. The failure to be simple.
2. The failure to be clear.
3. The failure to be direct.

Each failure can be overcome with short words, short sentences and short paragraphs . . . and the reader will understand what you have to say.

Talk directly to your reader. You know your customer, where he lives, where he works, his problems, hopes, dreams, worries, aspirations, goals. Think *one* customer. Have a clear picture of who he or she is and what he or she does.

Now, write to him.

Remember you are really a salesperson behind a computer instead of on a selling floor.

Remember your copy is a monologue instead of a dialogue. You are talking to a visualized but unseen audience you must grab and hold and make want to buy.

It is easier if you remember people buy for only one of two reasons. You offer a solution to a problem or a good feeling.

Writers often forget this basic rule: *Fear of loss is greater than promise of gain.*

There is so much emphasis placed on benefits to be gained and worries to be eased and health to be achieved and money to be made, we often overlook an even stronger emotion: the fear of losing a loved person or possession. (Which is why you see insurance as the number one item sold through the mails in the U.S.)

The finest writers in direct mail write with simplicity to people with all education levels. That's why it's called *Direct* mail.

"Then you should say what you mean," the March Hare went on.

"I do," Alice hastily replied: "at least I mean what I say. That's the same thing, you know."

"Not the same thing a bit!" said the Hatter. "Why, you might just as well say that 'I see what I eat' is the same thing as 'I eat what I see'!"

TOOLBOX

THE DOS AND DON'TS
OF DIRECT MAIL

MAKE SURE YOU DO . . .

1. Do write an outline, a guide to follow as-you write. Here's one: Headline — First paragraph — List of benefits — Proof of benefits — Reason to buy . . . now!

2. Do write to a friend . . . enthusiastically. Don't think of all your customers. Think of one. Write to that one. And *be enthusiastic!* Nothing sells merchandise as much as enthusiasm. Walter Chrysler once said he would pay more for an enthusiastic salesperson than a trained mechanic. And as long as you're writing to a friend, show the finished copy to a friend (relative, employee) before your direct mail piece is sent. What is *his* (or *her*) reaction?

3. Do write several headlines. Your odds of success increase the more headlines you write. And then pick and choose the one that tells and sells best. (For more on this, see Chapter 6, "Off With Their Heads!")

4. Do list benefits. Tell all the advantages. And disadvantages. (What happens to the customer if he does *not* buy?)

S. Do be specific. If you are selling a technical product, list the specifications. Great for those who want to know. Those who don't want to know will be impressed. Tell the reader *exactly* what they will receive.

6. Use the word "you." Here's an example of the use of the word "YOU" (the caps are ours) from a letter from the Book-of-the-Month Club:

Once YOU start shopping in America's Bookstore — YOU'LL be enjoying the most dependable reading reminder system in the world. YOU'LL be kept regularly informed of important new books, and given ample opportunity to choose the ones YOU want. YOU'LL soon come to depend on the Book-of-the-Month Club's thrifty shop-at-home service. Without leaving YOUR home, YOU can window-shop, browse and buy - and have the books YOU want delivered straight to YOUR door. And by continuing YOUR membership past the trial period, YOU'LL be eligible for our unique Book-Dividend plan.

7. Do write in the present tense. As much as possible. Things that are in the past are . . . in the past. Forgotten. A long time ago. Not pertinent to *today*. Be active, not passive.

8. Do write in simple phrases. Keep paragraphs short and sentences shorter.

9. Do include testimonials where possible. Every advertisement has the same problem: "Is it true?" If you say a fact about your product it means one thing. If a customer says the same fact, it is far more believable.

10. Do urge immediate action. Give a time when the offer ends. Tell them to come and try and see and, of course, buy. Hurry. Quick. Fast.

MAKE SURE YOU DON'T . . .

1. Don't wait for inspiration. Start writing by writing. When George Bernard Shaw was asked by a young man how to become a famous writer, Shaw answered, "Write." Sinclair Lewis said, "The art of writing is the art of applying the seat of the pants to the seat of the chair." So sit down and . . . write!

2. Don't exaggerate. L. L. Bean, founder of the famous catalog which bears his name, once advised, "Make sure the story isn't better than the store." His point: Don't stretch the facts. Just tell the advantages to the customer of buying your product. If the product seems even *better* than what you wrote, your next ad will be an even bigger success.

3. Don't use time-worn words. Avoid the circus adjectives of "outstanding," "terrific," "fantastic."

4. Don't use time-worn phrases. "Once in a lifetime," "red as a rose," and "clear as water" are old and will make your merchandise appear old. Exception: If you can re-phrase them in a fun way. We recently did a promotion of oversize clothing imported from Finland with the successful headline: "And now . . . the big Finnish!"

5. Don't patronize. Never imply you are doing the reader a favor by telling them about your product.

6. Don't make too many different offers in your mailing. Make your offer short, clear, understandable. If the reader cannot understand your offer, she will not respond.

7. Don't try to be funny. Humor is fine in a headline, in a TV sketch. But direct mail is different. It is very personal. That which makes you laugh may make your customer ask, "I wonder what they meant by that" or worse, consider your humor in bad taste.

8. Don't think of your direct mailer as just a direct mailer. Think of it as a salesman. Because . . . that's what it really is.

9. Don't assume everyone knows what you know. List all the facts even if you *think* your reader knows them. She will not mind being reminded.

10. Don't give up. Even if your last mailing piece did not do as well as you thought and/or hoped it would, the next one may do twice as well. The more you do, the more you will learn and the more comfortable you will feel about writing.

8

I'm Gonna Sit Right Down And Write Myself A Letter

Why do some letters work and others don't?

Bob Stone in his excellent book *Successful Direct Marketing Methods*. provides an answer with his seven-step formula.

1. Promise a benefit. Up front. Right in the beginning. Award-winning copywriter Bill Jayme asks,

"Does the lead on your letter say 'Read me because'?"

What positive event will happen to the reader who keeps on reading?

2. Enlarge on the benefit. The opening benefit is short, concise, summarized. It could be a headline on the top of the letter. It could be a strong, attention-demanding first paragraph.

Now, the next few paragraphs explain in greater detail what is included in this benefit.

3. Be specific. The best way to explain this is to have you look at a Sears catalog. Descriptions of merchandise are short and concise but they tell you what you want to know. Colors. Sizes. Washable? Price. Does it work in 20-below weather?

4. Give proof. Testimonials are good. And not necessarily only from famous people. A testimonial from a real person in your community is believable and adds credibility to your offer.

5. What happens if they don't act. Remember fear of loss is a great motivator. That's why there is so much insurance sold. And that is the reason cut-off dates are important in your letter. They spur the customer to immediate action. Phrases like, "The free camera is yours only if you act before ..." are powerful involvement tools.

6. Repeat. The close of the sale. Where the salesperson summarizes and repeats all the benefits of buying he listed during the entire sales talk. Short, concise and gives reasons for buying... *now!*

7. AFTO. The salesman's critical concluding phrase: Ask For The Order.

Tell the customer what to do. "Cut along this line." "Print your name here." "Fold and seal." "Please check appropriate payment box: American Express, Visa, MasterCard, Diner's Club, Check ..."

After you master the basics of writing a letter, you graduate to the next step, the putting together of a direct mail *package*. **The letter is the most important element in the package**. But a direct mail package has five different parts.

FIVE "GIVENS" FOR A SUCCESSFUL DIRECT MAIL PACKAGE

1. The outside envelope.
• What have you **given** me to make me want to open and read more?
2. The letter.
• What have you **given** me to make me want to keep on reading?
3. The brochure.
• What have you **given** me so that I can read more about your offer?
4. The order blank.
• What have you **given** me so I can buy now ... at once?
5. The return envelope.
• What have you **given** me to make it easy to send you back the order?
(On a business reply card, combine *4* and *5*.)

Let's look at them one by one:
1. The outside envelope. Almost all of your packages can be mailed third class in large quantities. They should because of the savings in

postage and because readership has little or no relationship to whether you mail first class or third class.

You can use a window envelope. This way the person's name shows through (which means it does not have to be repeated on the envelope).

You can use questions on the envelope, each written to appeal in some manner. At least one will make the reader ask, "Hmmmm, what is the answer to *that* question?"

2. The letter. Start with the "headline." The catch word or phrase to be printed in big letters or color.

The first paragraph should give you the complete message of the entire letter.

The rest of the letter enlarges on the benefit you offer in the first paragraph.

Different paragraph indenting breaks up the page. Makes it more interesting to read.

End your letter with a signature (signed in blue) and a P.S. special offer (Example: send money with order and receive free issues).

3. The brochure. Describe your product or service more fully. Use illustrations or photographs. The brochure is for information that will stay the same for a number of years (because a brochure can be expensive to print). For items that change (such as pricing) consider a tuck-in price list.

The publishers letter. This little fold-over piece of paper adds less than a penny to the cost of your package and means an automatic increase in replies. The name "publisher's letter" first came about because it was used by book publishers to give you one more reason you should buy their books. (It's also called a "lift" letter because it lifts results.) The opening line is always similar to this one: "DON'T BOTHER TO READ THIS unless you're not sure about accepting the proposal" with someone's name or initials inside. The copy stresses one more reason to buy from an officer of the company or well-known person.

4. The order blank. This is a summary of everything you have put in your letter. Here you can pick up the *free* offer and make it a tear-off piece on the end of the Business Reply Card. A headline could be helpful here.

Repeat the."extra" benefit on the order blank. Example: Two free issues if they send in check with order.

Remember: Your order blank is your last-minute salesman.

So tell your reader exactly what to do. Be specific. Give specific instructions on mailing the reply card or using an 800 number. If you've included an involvement device, say how to punch out the token or remove the label and where to place it before responding.

Describe exactly how you want the reply card filled And tell the reader to "cut along this line" and "print your name here' and "put stamp here…"

5. The business reply envelope. All they have to do now is check what they want on the order blank, tuck it into the envelope and toss it in the nearest mailbox. No writing. No stamp-putting-on. Make it easy for your customers to respond.

TYPES OF LETTERS

The most important part of your direct mail package is your letter.

Up until now, you probably thought a letter was a letter.

Not really. There are many different ways to write your letter to make it different, unique, stand out and in front of all the other letters received in the morning mail.

Here are examples of letters that worked for us and others. Ideas you could adapt and adopt for yourself:

The Marketing to Your Market Letter

The first rule of any kind of advertising is to remember it is far, far easier to sell more to the customer you have than to sell a new customer. This is an axiom that is made for direct marketing.

The following three letters prove that point.

1. The Bank Letter. A small bank was losing money in New York

City. The bank president's problem: How could he compete with the giants? He decided to contact only the people in his neighborhood, which was only a small part of New York City.

2. *The Insurance Letter.* The problem: insurance companies all came out with a new low-premium policy for non smokers. How could this one agent let his non smoking customers become aware of this new low premium before they went to another company?

3. *The Supermarket Letter.* The problem: how to contact the new people who move into a community and have them buy groceries from you? If one out of five people moves every year, is there a way to contact the new people?

The Bank Letter

The bank was one of the smallest in New York City, and it wanted to increase its deposits. Chelsea National Bank president Merton Corn knew what he could not do. He could not afford to advertise on TV. He could not afford to advertise in *The New York Times.* He could not afford to advertise on the New York City radio stations top-rated drive time. He could not afford to advertise in the magazines in New York City. However, he could afford direct mail.

He drew a circle around his bank located just below Central Park in Manhattan. He said this "community" within the circle was the "city" where his bank was located. Then he began his direct marketing advertising campaign.

He put together a series of letters, each aimed at a different market.

- Firefighters and police officers inside the circle received letters at their station or precinct houses. Their checks were issued twice a month. Why take them home? Why not simply deposit them in the nearby Chelsea Bank? Corn knew that the main reason people choose a particular bank is convenience. He would take this advantage and make it work for him.

- Current depositors received letters offering incentives if they opened additional accounts with the bank. If you had a minimum savings account, you also could have "free checking." The more accounts customers have with a bank, the less likely they are to switch banks. If a customer has a savings account, the odds are 2 to 1 he or she will not leave before the end of the year. If the customer has a checking and savings account, the odds jump to 10 to 1; if the customer has three accounts, the odds are 25 to 1. If the customer has four accounts, the odds go to 100 to 1. Corn wanted not only to attract new depositors, but also to increase the accounts held by current customers.

• Corporate personal accounts. Corn wrote letters to companies that borrowed from the bank for their businesses, asking if they would also like to have a personal account in the bank. At the end of this letter, he added the postscript (the best read part of any letter): "We will, of course, try to show our appreciation for this expression of confidence in us." If you were borrowing large sums of money for your business and the president of the bank wrote you asking for a personal account, would you oblige? How fast?

• President to president, Corn wrote the small businesses in his newly formed "circle city." His opening line was, "You're the president of a small business. I'm the president of a small bank. Why don't we get together and talk president to president." The implication was that the small business person might have a difficult time if he or she called Chase Manhattan and wanted to talk about business problems with Chase's president. But there was a bank president, Merton Corn, ready and willing.

This letter campaign attracted so much attention that the headline was picked up and used by banks across the country as a way to increase their corporate business. Business jumped at the Chelsea Bank in both dollars and customers, all because of an advertising campaign that was limited to direct marketing.

On the next page is the text of the letter which was sent out:

Dear   ,

I want to offer you a better banking deal than I think you have now because we are a small bank, located nearby; we are anxious to attract depositors such as yourself.

We have the following things to offer which we think will be of interest

1. No-charge checking accounts if you maintain a $500 savings account with us. We pay the maximum interest rate allowed by law for commercial banks from day of deposit to day of withdrawal.

2. Long hours - 8:30 a.m. to 5:00 p.m., Monday through Friday.

3. We have special free checking accounts for senior citizens.

4, We would be happy to arrange with the Department of Health, Education and Welfare; Social Security Administration, for direct deposit of any social security checks to our bank, saving you time and effort in making deposits.

5. We have a large supply of safe deposit boxes in which to store your valuables.

I am enclosing signature cards for savings and checking accounts and a postage paid envelope for your convenience. If you prefer, stop in and say hello to our Branch Manager.

Sincerely yours,

President

P.S. If you have any questions, please do not hesitate to call me.

The Insurance Letter

Jerry Rimm sells insurance in southern New Jersey. As an independent agent, he has a limited advertising budget.

One of his firms, Philadelphia Life Insurance Company, came out with a new policy for non smokers. The premiums were reduced drastically. A non smoker could nearly double the insurance coverage at about the same price. The company's brochure was full of facts, figures, and numbers. It was nearly impossible to read.

"How many customers do you have under the letter "A" that you think can use this new policy?" we asked.

About thirty or so," said Rimm.

"Would you spend $10 on a direct mail campaign?"

"Ten dollars? Sure!"

He then mailed the thirty customers a letter. The outside of the envelope said, "For you a non smoker." Inside, he enclosed the fact-filled, data-packed brochure from the insurance company. He also attached a small handwritten note personalized for each of the thirty customers. It said:

Dear (customer's name):

Now for the first time you, as a non-smoker, can have $100,000 of life insurance for only $514 ($500,000 for $2,000).

The enclosed folder has the facts and figures. Call me today at 555-5201.

Jerry

Note the personalization from the name to the specific amount (because Rimm knew the customer's age) and the add-on suggested sale for the increased coverage. Within 72 hours, he sold more than $2 million of life insurance.

Ben Feldman's Story

There are more than 1,600 life insurance companies in America. Ben Feldman is one of the nation's top salesmen. By himself, he has written more insurance than 1,000 of the companies! He was the first insurance salesman to pass the goal of $25 million in one year.

And then doubled that figure.

Ben has been a leading salesman for New York Life for more than four decades. He set these records in a little town on the Ohio River: East Liverpool, population about 20,000.

What is the secret of his success?

"Three things," says Ben.

"1. Work hard.

"2. Think big.

"3. Listen very well."

How he parlays each of these goals into million-dollar sales would take several chapters to describe. But he does use one indispensable marketing tool that helps him attain and exceed his own records: direct mail letters.

His letters are short, to the point and immediately visible. Here's an example:

Dear (customer's name):

Will you trade one hour of your time for $1.00 each day for the rest of your life?

On July 14th, your insurance rates go up $1.00 per day forever.

Best wishes.

Ben Feldman.

The dates are from a private "birthday book" he keeps on his customers.

Once a month he mails out about twenty of these letters with a brand new dollar bill pinned to each one.

Results: "These letters result in policies of six and sometimes seven figures."

The Supermarket Letter

If you are newly married, or moving to rural southwestern Wisconsin, the odds are you will food shop at Dick's supermarkets.

The 35-year-old, five-store supermarket chain captures the major share of the retail food dollars in their market with direct mail.

Their mail promotion began about twenty years ago, says President William Brodbeck, and it is still going strong.

Here's how it works:

1. The Lists. Store personnel put together three lists daily:

The newly arrived: who just moved into any shopping area with a Dick's supermarket. These names come from utilities, chambers of commerce, newspapers, and personal knowledge.

The newly married: Names culled from the society pages of the area newspapers.

The newly born: from birth announcements.

2. The Letters. The first two groups receive a letter from the manager of their nearest Dick's supermarket. He welcomes them to the community. He tells about Dick's. He lists the benefits and special features of his store.

3. The Offer. Included with each letter are six different coupons. Each is good for one free food item. One coupon redeemable each week for six consecutive weeks.

The coupons are for wanted merchandise: a five-pound bag of Idaho potatoes, a pound of cottage cheese, a dozen eggs, a half gallon of milk. All free.

4. The Next Letter. Bill Brodbeck writes a follow-up note about three weeks later, as President of Dick's. (How does he know they came? He doesn't bother to check since **90 percent of all mailed coupons were used!**)

He asks these new buyers a favor. Since they are now customers of Dick's, they can help the store do an even better job by simply answering the questions in the enclosed questionnaire, with a stamped, self-addressed envelope.

And, oh yes, for taking the time to answer the questionnaire, Dick's has included for you another six free food coupons to use, one a week for the next six weeks.

5. The Follow-Up. One year later this "new" customer has become a "steady" customer. Time for a new questionnaire based on the customer's experience with the store over the year. A follow-up file tells the Dick's secretary when the year has gone by. For taking the time to answer the questions, Dick's has enclosed for you a coupon for free goods at their bakery department.

6. The Results: Customers feel they are part of the Dick's family. The communities where Dick's stores are located are all small (population varies from 2,400 to 9,500). Everyone knows everyone. And everyone knows, respects and simply likes to shop at Dick's.

Customers also see their comments on the questionnaires put into action. ("We get back more than 85 percent of the questionnaires we send out," says Brodbeck. "And we read each one of them for ideas and suggestions.")

One repeated suggestion was a preference for bulk produce instead of pre-packaged. (Translation: you can pick and choose and hold and feel and examine each apple, orange, grape, tomato, instead of having them pre-packaged and pre-selected and pre-priced by the store.) Dick's switched to what the customers wanted. Sales increased!

The other value of the questionnaire: cross-selling. When a customer is asked an opinion on the photo finishing service or recipe cards ("Do you pick up our recipe cards each week?"), some never knew, until that moment, the store had photo finishing service and recipe cards. The questionnaire became a selling tool, a subconscious reminder "If this is what you want to buy we have it, folks.")

The third mailer is the most recent in their promotion. This letter goes to the newborn babies. The names are sent to Dick's by local hospitals. This letter is addressed to the baby by name with a $2.00 coupon "for your parents to use" for any baby product from food to clothing to accessories.

One year later, the baby receives another letter with congratulations on his or her birthday and, ah, yes, a coupon for 25 percent off that first birthday cake from the bakery department.

(See one of Dick's letters superimposed with coupons on the next page)

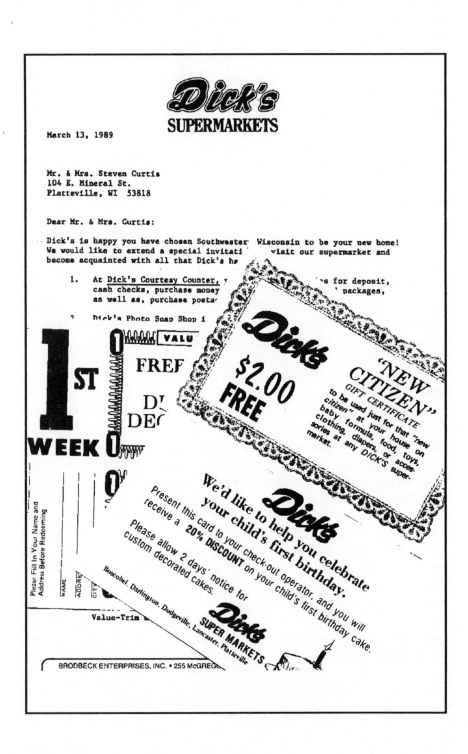

Dick's
SUPERMARKETS

March 13, 1989

Mr. & Mrs. Steven Curtis
104 E. Mineral St.
Platteville, WI 53818

Dear Mr. & Mrs. Curtis:

Dick's is happy you have chosen Southwester Wisconsin to be your new home!
We would like to extend a special invitati   visit our supermarket and
become acquainted with all that Dick's ha

1. At Dick's Courtesy Counter,   s for deposit,
    cash checks, purchase money   ' packages,
    as well as, purchase posta

2. Dick's Photo Snap Shop i

1ST
WEEK
VALU
FREF
D'
DE(

Please: Fill In Your Name and
Address Before Redeeming

NAME
ADDRE
CITY

Value-Trim

We'd like to help you celebrate
your child's first birthday.
Present this card to your check-out operator, and you will
receive a **20% DISCOUNT** on your child's first birthday cake.
Please allow 2 days' notice for
custom decorated cakes.

Boscobel, Darlington, Dudgeville, Lancaster, Platteville

Dick's
SUPER MARKETS

Dick's
$2.00
FREE

"NEW CITIZEN"
GIFT CERTIFICATE
to be used just for that "new
citizen" at your house on
baby formula, food, toys,
clothing, diapers, and accessories at any DICK'S supermarket.

BRODBECK ENTERPRISES, INC. • 255 McGREG

When we asked what changes were made in the program in the years since it began, Brodbeck answered, "Very few." "If Dick's opens a new department in a particular store, we add that information to the letter. But the copy has not changed. And the food items have not changed."

The original choice of giving away basic food items is as strong today as the day the first mailing went out. "We wanted items to have universal appeal with the highest usage. What worked when we first tried it still works today," Brodbeck says.

Remember: the letters, while not changing, are really new to the customer receiving them for the first time. To Dick's it is the same letter as mailed a decade ago. To the person receiving the letter, it is as fresh, interesting and up-to-date as the morning's newspaper.

Does Bill Brodbeck recommend this direct mail program for other food retailers? Yes! "It's an excellent way to encourage the customer to shop your store on multiple occasions. The value of the free coupons almost guarantees what will happen."

The trick of course is to catch the customer before he or she start a habit pattern by shopping a competitive store. Brodbeck adds, "By attracting these new customers to our store early, we have a great opportunity to convince them our store is the store they ought to shop."

A few years ago, addressing the Food Marketing Institute's national convention of thousands of retail food stores from all over the United States, Brodbeck talked about his store saying, "Our reputation rests on a very open relationship with our customers. We do our best to communicate with them often and in meaningful ways."

That basic philosophy is behind this very successful direct mail campaign. "Above all," he sums up, "we must keep the communications open with our customers."

This well-coordinated, thought-out and carefully followed-through direct mail program is a guide for any merchant in any business. It is also a reminder that the customer not only has to be originally sought but must also be continually looked after and listened to.

The Headline Letter

We find this approach works well for us. Perhaps because we are print oriented. We look for the appealing headline for an advertisement on the outside of the envelope. What group of words will capture the readers' interest and make them want to keep on reading?

Instead of using those words and/or phrases in the opening *sentence,* why not use them up there on top of the letter? All capital letters. Flush left. Or centered. Underlined. Double-spaced. Or in a box.

- *Eliminates a personal greeting.* You can type in the person's name, title, address as shown, but you do not have to repeat the name if you have a headline.
- *Sets the tone immediately.* The reader knows at once what the letter is all about. The whole concept is digested into the headline.
- *Gives you breathing room to write.* After you have captured the reader's interest with the headline, the customer will keep on reading to find out what the headline means. This means you can go into more detail about your merchandise/ product/offer *before* explaining what the headline is all about.

Which brings us to the letter we wrote for the Alley Deli in our shopping center. They were about to open but had little money left for advertising. We suggested they simply ...write a letter!

RESULTS

ALLEY DELI

This letter was sent by a new small restaurant to influential people in the community: elected officials, prominent businessmen, professionals. Purpose: to build customers, make them aware the restaurant was open. Cost was minimal. For 100 letters, postage and typing -- under $50.

Reaction was excellent. More than half took advantage of the free sandwich. And most ordered *at least one more* sandwich.

Within a month, half were steady come-in or call-up customers.

With a very, very small budget, the use of this letter achieved maximum results.

(The Alley Deli letter, which appears on the next page, was selected by Dick Hodgson for his book, *The Greatest Direct Mail Sales Letters of All Time.*)

THE PRESIDENTIAL CARD (AUSTRALIA)

When we met Tony Ingleton of Melbourne, Australia, at the Pan Pacific Direct Marketing Symposium in Sydney in 1981, we were impressed with his new Presidential Card program. It offered members an opportunity to save money on hotel rooms, restaurant meals, rent-a-car and other expenses.

We examined his entire mailing program. We suggested new ways to promote not only his *new* membership but also how to re-activate members who did *not* renew.

We wrote several letters for Tony:

1. For new members.

2. For members who did not respond to the first request for renewal (a reminder letter).

3. For members who did not renew, a reason for renewing six months down the road.

Because of his letters . . .

1. Membership doubled.

2. Retention rate doubled. (Because the customer was contacted again if he did not respond the first time around . . .)

Today, more than 100,000 Australians belong to the Presidential Card with more signing up at a rate nearly double the rate of a few years ago. This success is due mainly to the letters since they are his major form of advertising.

One of the more successful Presidential Card letters opened with

the alley deli

Gordon's Alley, Atlantic City, N.J.
Established 1984. Proprietor: Norman Gordon
Take out & delivery service: 345-1060

Murray Raphel
12 S. Virginia Ave.
Atlantic City, NJ 08401
October 2, 1992

**WHOEVER SAID THERE'S NO SUCH THING AS A
FREE LUNCH DIDN'T KNOW ABOUT THIS LETTER.**

Good morning, Mr. Raphel:

Let me introduce myself. My name is Norman Gordon and I own the
Alley Deli in Gordon's Alley.

And if you've ever wondered whatever happened to the good old
fashioned (and delicious) deli sandwich, well, there's good news this
morning: those sandwiches are back. Here. In my deli.

I've enclosed a copy of our menu. I'm real proud of the excellent
quality and superb taste of everything we have. (I cook the roast beef
and turkey fresh every day). And I want you share the good times with
me. And so I've enclosed a gift certificate for a free lunch.

Whoever said there's no such thing as a free lunch?

There is. For you. From me.

Enjoy!

Norman Gordon

P.S. If you think there's some secret gimmick here, you're right. I'm so
convinced you'll enjoy eating in my deli that you'll come back again
and again and again.

P.P.S. If you're real busy and can't come to the deli, let us bring the deli
to you. Call us at 345-1060 or fax us at 347-2455 and your order is on
its way. Have your gift certificate ready when we arrive.

the following headline: "Would you buy $900 worth of services for $69?" We have found that putting the potential dollar savings of your product or service immediately attracts the reader's attention. In the case of the Presidential Card, that headline resulted in a 50 percent increase in the amount of people renewing their membership in the Card from the previous year's campaign. (The opening page of The Presidential Card letter is reproduced on the following page.)

The Tell-the-World Letter

You've seen this as an ad that usually begins, "An open letter to . . " (Fill in the blank with the audience you are trying to reach.)

What it does: Takes the intimacy of a letter and captures *some* of the same personal relationship on a large scale. True, the letter is now written to everyone instead of someone but results can be dramatic.

Banks did this very effectively when Congress decided to tax your interest on savings by having banks withhold the taxes. Banks ran sample letters in newspapers all over America asking people to use these letters to write their Congressmen to repeal the law.

Millions wrote. The law was repealed. The mass letter worked.

Special interest groups use this same approach when they want you to communicate with a decision-maker. The back page of the Sunday *New York Times* often has a letter from one of these groups asking you to write in support of their cause.

This letter has the advantage of:

- *Mass audience.* You reach a lot of people . . . and quickly.
- *Massive response.* If you touch the right emotional response, the response can be overwhelming and immediate.

The Newsweek subscription letter.

Nearly 107 million of these letters were mailed out by *Newsweek!*
The letter was written by direct mail expert Ed McLean.
Before Ed tells us why it worked so well, count the number of

Please address all general correspondence to:
P.O. Box 3042, Grenfell Street, Adelaide 5000
Adelaide Office: 20 Hindmarsh Square, Adelaide 5000
Next to the Academy Cinema
Telephone: (08) 223 1722
Melbourne Office: P.O. Box 172, Toorak 3142
Telephone Toll Free: (008) 886314
Fax: (08) 223 5838

Mr. Ian Kennedy
111 Bond Street
Sydney, New South Wales

Tony Ingleton
President

WOULD YOU BUY $900 WORTH OF SERVICES FOR $69?

Sure.

Why not?
Who wouldn't?
That's exactly how R.A. Judge in Chapman A.C.T. feels.
Here's what he wrote to us:

"Our savings (as Presidential Card members) so far this year are over $900 which is about our usual situation."

The most important phrase in that sentence is NOT the $900 savings. The most important phrase is "which is about our usual situation."

A week does not go by without someone writing in to tell us how much they save as Presidential Card members.

Here's another one from Ms. M. Kalwiski, Highgate Hill, Queensland:

"I just returned from a two- week driving vacation in N.S.W. and was able to save $285 which is terrific."

And when you figure how much she is saving over the course of the year, the $69 investment seems like a very good deal, indeed.

Which it is.

And that is the reason for us writing to you today. Your Presidential Card has expired. Send in your renewal at once to continue receiving your savings on hotel rooms, dining and entertainment.

(Please turn the page for THE BEST NEWS OF ALL)

times he uses the word "You." It's at least 27 times on just this *first* page. (See the first page of the Newsweek subscription letter on the next page.)

"It was the first direct mail piece I ever wrote," says Ed. "It was in 1960. When I came to work old timers told me there was only one way to sell subscriptions to *Newsweek* and that was with colorful, expensive mailing pieces. I looked over what they did and knew why I never subscribed to *Newsweek*. The copy was full of slogans and claims, few of them with any supporting material.

"I read through several years of the magazine — a practice I still follow today when creating a subscription letter — and got a 'feel' for what the editors were trying to do. I had been a salesman, selling door to door and I always tried to catch the housewife's attention and interest quickly. If I didn't, I would fail.

"Applying this to *Newsweek* subscription direct mail, I set out to capture the reader's attention in the first paragraph. As someone new to direct mail, I was curious about mailing lists and I suspected other people were, too. So I started in what I thought was a straightforward manner, acknowledging the fact that we had found the reader's name on a mailing list of affluent people.

"Then I sold the value of being well informed, which is a key benefit. And this led to a discussion of some features which *Newsweek* would likely cover. I sensed that people subscribed to a news magazine for the future, not for the present or past. And I found out that this was so: trial subscriptions to *Time* and *Newsweek* are easier to sell just before a national election or other major event.

"The letter cost less than one-half of what the control cost and produced twice as many orders.

"This letter was the *Newsweek* control for nearly twenty years, until a free calculator offer beat it. I have been told that nearly 107 million copies of the letter were mailed before it was retired."

Begin with a story.

That's what copywriter Ed McLean did in his letter for Xerox Learning Systems. Remember how Bill Jayme said he had to "become the reader"? McLean does the same thing here. A story

Newsweek

NEWSWEEK • 117 EAST THIRD STREET • DAYTON 2, OHIO

Dear Reader:

If the list upon which I found your name is any indication, this is not the first — nor will it be the last — subscription letter you receive. Quite frankly, your education and income set you apart from the general population and make you a highly-rated prospect for everything from magazines to mutual funds.

You've undoubtedly 'heard everything' by now in the way of promises and premiums. I won't try to top any of them.

Nor will I insult your intelligence.

If you subscribe to Newsweek, you won't get rich quick. You won't bowl over friends and business associates with clever remarks and sage comments after your first copy of Newsweek arrives. (Your conversation will benefit from a better understanding of the events and forces of our era, but that's all. Wit and wisdom are gifts no magazine can bestow.) And should you attain further professional or business success during the term of your subscription, you'll have your own native ability and good luck to thank for it — not Newsweek.

What, then, can Newsweek do for you?

The answer depends upon what type of person you happen to be. If you are not curious about what's going on outside your own immediate daily range of concern . . . if you are quickly bored when the topic of conversation shifts from your house, your car, your ambitions . . . if you couldn't care less about what's happening in Washington or Wall Street, in London or Moscow . . . then forget Newsweek. It can't do a thing for you.

If, on the other hand, you are the kind of individual who

opening is a good opening because it immediately captures the reader's interest:

Xerox Learning Systems
Depot Square
PO Box 825
Peterborough, NH 03458

XEROX

Dear Executive:

Fresh out of college, he started at the financial services company as a management trainee at $200 a week.

That was nine years ago. Now, a string of promotions and several substantial salary increases later, he heads up one of the corporation's major profit centers, with over a hundred people under him.

A first-rate idea person, he looks for imaginative solutions to business challenges.

He gets in at nine, uses his time well, and rarely stays after five. At least one day a week he takes an early train home — "to think and plan," he says.

His desk isn't always free of papers but it's cleared before he leaves. He's punctual, well-organized, effective in meetings. Yet those around him call him low-keyed, even a bit laid-back.

What's more important: at age 33 he feels good about himself, his job, his life, his future. By next year, if another firm hasn't made him an irresistible offer, he'll be ready for new and larger responsibilities within the company.

An unusual person? Not really. In my work I see many men and women in management who function as well as this man does.

My name is John J. Franco. I am President of a division of Xerox Corporation known as Xerox Learning Systems. Our business is helping people do a better job. We serve thousands of corporations, including 417 of the Fortune 500.

Recently, a number of our clients asked us to help them find out why some executives seem to handle their jobs with ease while others, just as bright and talented, must work harder and longer to achieve the same result.

Please Fold, Tear, Spindle, Staple or Mutilate

The next time you use the mail for sales, try stapling, pinning or clipping an attachment to your letter. Try attaching a note and/or change the color of the paper or ink. Try an unusual fold that produces a progressive disclosure technique -- that means you read only small parts of the copy with each fold. Folds can simulate the opening of curtains, doors or windows. Fan folds are always attention getters. Use your imagination. Chances are that your competitor could care less about how *his* mailing is folded.

We even mutilated a mailing to attract attention. For a fund-raising letter, we actually had part of the mailing burned, asking for contributions to pay off the mortgage which they could then burn up. (Yes, there are suppliers who will scorch or burn the edges of your mailing piece.)

Inexpensive slitting or die cuts have unlimited possibilities. In a mailing for a Columbus Day Sale, we put a slit in a picture of a bottle floating in the ocean. Stuffed in the slit was a separate note which could be pulled out of the bottle.

The P.S. is at the . . . beginning of the letter?

Since it is a well-known fact that the P.S. is one of the best-read parts of a letter, this one *begins* with the P.S.

A certain attention-grabber, this P.S. explains why it is placed at the beginning, follows that with a major benefit and follows that by . . . the *beginning* of the letter. (See the Esquire letter next page).

"Flashers" Attract Attention

We've been stumped! For a long time we've been trying to find a word, just the right word, to describe all of the little graphic nuances that can make a direct mail letter more effective. Now we think we have found that word. It's "flashers." Flashers seems the right word because flashers of any kind attract attention and that's what we want them to do in our direct mail letters.

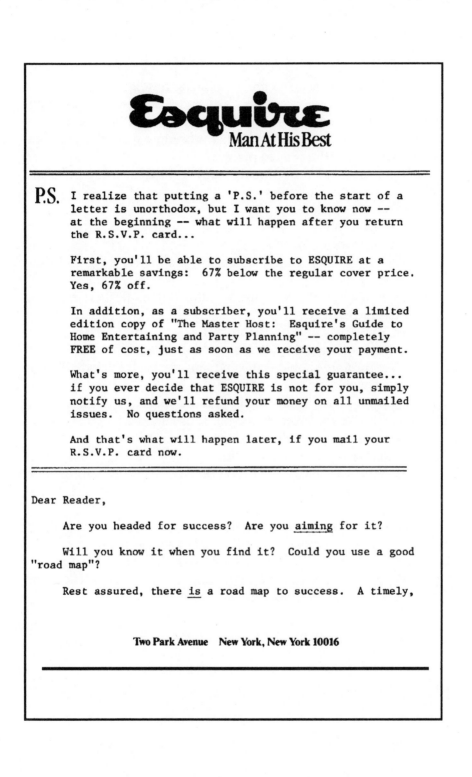

Esquire
Man At His Best

P.S. I realize that putting a 'P.S.' before the start of a letter is unorthodox, but I want you to know now -- at the beginning -- what will happen after you return the R.S.V.P. card...

First, you'll be able to subscribe to ESQUIRE at a remarkable savings: 67% below the regular cover price. Yes, 67% off.

In addition, as a subscriber, you'll receive a limited edition copy of "The Master Host: Esquire's Guide to Home Entertaining and Party Planning" -- completely FREE of cost, just as soon as we receive your payment.

What's more, you'll receive this special guarantee... if you ever decide that ESQUIRE is not for you, simply notify us, and we'll refund your money on all unmailed issues. No questions asked.

And that's what will happen later, if you mail your R.S.V.P. card now.

Dear Reader,

Are you headed for success? Are you <u>aiming</u> for it?

Will you know it when you find it? Could you use a good "road map"?

Rest assured, there <u>is</u> a road map to success. A timely,

Two Park Avenue   New York, New York 10016

I'm Gonna Sit Right Down and Write Myself A Letter / 111

One of our favorite flashers is <u>underlining,</u> a way of calling attention to key points. Straight underlining has been popular since the beginning of direct mail and mail-order copywriting, but now there is a new approach — highlighting with color, just as students do in textbooks. It's a simple printing procedure that adds only one additional color to the printed piece.

Indenting is an often overlooked copy technique. It is particularly appropriate when you want to:

1. List features or benefits.
2. Sub-paragraph.
3. Break up long copy.

Some copywriters routinely indent copy on every page to insure easier reading.

[Brackets may be the least used of the various flashers but they offer a change of pace.]

Don't overlook handwritten notes . . . they really work! Handwritten notes not only attract attention but also lend a personal touch to copy. Care should be taken to insure that the handwriting is completely legible.

Using lines to completely box-in portions of your letter is another version of the brackets technique but is usually reserved for special offers, conditions, guarantees or instructions. The box is most often used in combination with indentation.

Simulated rubber stamp impressions find applications for such things as calling attention to expiration dates of your direct mail offers.

Check marks, bullets and parentheses can also be used to break up long copy, as they help to keep the reader's attention.

Using a different color for any of our flashers adds to their effectiveness and makes for a more graphically pleasing letter. The most popular alternate colors are blue and red.

9

YOUR FUTURE IS IN THE CARDS!

POSTCARDS HAVE COME a long way since they were introduced in Austria in 1869 as straw-colored pieces of board called Korrespondenz Karte.

But they still perform the same service: telling someone else you were thinking of them and took the time to write and say so.

Our preferred customers receive postcards from us when we travel. Not the usual "wish you were here" but a selling message or an explanation of why we are *there*.

Most times we arrange to have a few dozen (or a few hundred) cards sent to us ahead of time with scenes indigenous to the country we are going to visit. We write and address the cards *before* we leave, take them with us and mail them from the country when we arrive.

Or we take pretyped name and address peel-off labels, buy the appropriate cards and every day write ten or more cards telling our best customers that we are thinking of them *wherever* we are.

We have written from Australia and Helsinki and London and Paris and Stockholm and Singapore and Hong Kong and Copenhagen.

We have written from the Grand Canyon and Yellowstone and Denver and Disneyland and New Orleans and Chicago and Boston and New York City.

These postcards carry a sales message but with the impact of an intimate person-to-person contact from a far-off place. And when we get back home, people actually thank us for sending them direct mail!

The postcard may be one of direct mail's most neglected techniques. Too frequently we overlook its many advantages, its versatility and the countless opportunities for its use.

Postcards are inexpensive.

They can be printed with any color ink, combinations of colors, on different color stock or in full color.

They can be designed in many sizes and shapes.

They can carry something other than the message. (More about this later.)

They require minimum amount of copy or graphics.

And above all, (probably because of their "greetings" origin), postcards enjoy a very personal image.

Almost any marketing program can take advantage of postcards. Use picture postcards for new product introductions, particularly for products inconvenient for a salesperson to carry. Use postcards to announce a sale. (Big postcard for big sales?)

Use postcards to introduce a new salesman in a territory with his picture on one side of the card and a short "bio" on the other side.

Use postcards to build traffic at meetings, seminars and trade shows.

Postcards are a quick way to call attention to an address or telephone number change. An accounting service in Hawaii sends out a combined New Year's card and tax season message and receives about a 15 percent *client* return!

We recently received a full color card with a picture of a crocus peeking out of the snow. The card was mailed from Breck in Holland announcing their annual tulip bulb sale.

Our favorite postcard story: There's a family who live in the pine forest of southern New Jersey on the road to the popular seashore resorts. During the winter, they scrawl notes on postcards offering free pickup of unwanted major appliances. These are mailed to a list of vacation homeowners. Many part time residents decide to buy new appliances when they arrive at their summer homes but find it difficult to get rid of the old refrigerators and stoves. The note-writer comes in with his truck, picks up the old appliances and takes them to an open area in the woods facing one of the major highways leading to the resort.

His hand-painted FOR SALE sign attracts those who own rental units at the seashore. After a long, cold winter, they often have to replace inexpensive appliances for their tenants. Here's a successful small business, started by someone who uses a simple postcard to bring in, free, the products he sells.

Postcards are not restricted to one-way messages. They can be used as order cards to be filled in and returned in an envelope. Or as folded business reply cards. And for something really creative, *Penthouse* magazine attached a letter in an envelope to a giant postcard and gained the best of both worlds: They had the impact of the picture postcard along with the long copy and order form included in the attached envelope.

Recently a company came up with a postcard that contains a peel-off self-adhesive sticker that can be used as a miniature bumper sticker or label.

Another company perforates a picture postcard in the shape of the standard rotary telephone index. When torn from the postcard, the card contains a portion of the picture from the postcard on one side and the printed name, address and phone information on the reverse side. It's a unique way to get your name and message onto someone's desk file.

Here's an easy-to-understand message from our local insurance agent that convinced us to arrange a meeting with him.

Postcards are an easy, simple and uncomplicated way for you to begin doing your direct mail.

Just sit down at your desk, pre-select some of your best customers and drop them a note about what you have for them that's new or on sale, or simply say you are thinking of them. (Few people do *that.*)

If what you want to say, offer or sell takes up more room than available on a postcard, it's time to move up to the next generation. The self-mailer. No envelope to open. Just unfold once or several times and read all about it . . .

THE BARE FACTS: DIRECT MAIL UNCOVERED

The simple fold-over mailers we used for our New Year's Sale for our shops in Atlantic City were the same size, shape and look for twenty five years. *And each one brought in more business that one day than we do most other **weeks** of the year.*

We bring this to your attention at this point to emphasize the importance of self-mailers. They go it alone. And are very effective.

Look through your morning mail. Most are self-mailers. That means they are complete unto themselves. No envelope, no brochure, no special insert. What you see is what you get.

Postcards are one example. But the message is out for everyone to see.

Self-mailers are most often folded with the message *inside,* and you open, turn, unfold to read because the headline makes you open, turn or unfold to read.

Self-mailers are typically folders, booklets, brochures, newsletters, circulars and catalogs.

HERE ARE THE ADVANTAGES OF SELF-MAILERS:

1. They are less expensive. (No envelope costs.)
2. They are easy to open. (No ripping of an envelope.)
3. They are easy to read. (The headline makes you open the first fold which makes you interested enough to unfold the next fold which . . .)

4. You can use the same address for going to the customer and coming *back* to you (See examples at end of this chapter.)

5. The response device (that means an order card or business reply card or coupon for you to use when you shop) is right there in front of you.

HERE IS SOME MORE INFORMATION ABOUT SELF-MAILERS:

1. There is limited space for a detailed story or offer.

2. It says, "Hi there, folks. I'm an advertisement!" Which *can* be an advantage. For if the customer *knows* what it is and you have interested them enough to open and read, you are halfway home.

Here are some examples of self-mailers we all receive:

• *Marketing the Market.* You are the proud owner of a new computer. You promptly fill in and mail your registration/guarantee card. Your name is sold as part of a mailing list of computer owners to a computer magazine. They send you a self-mailer. The teaser copy on the front says, "Congratulations! Your new [brand name] computer opens a wide world of information to you. And [name of magazine] helps you explore this exciting new world." The back of the self-mailer is filled with covers of recent issues of the magazine. Without opening an envelope . . . without removing a staple . . . without breaking a seal, you find tantalizing copy and graphics with just a simple unfolding. Right audience. Right offer. Right format.

• *Trading Up to the Trade.* "Coming to Philadelphia for the first time — a seminar for Manufacturers' Representatives" reads the teaser copy.

The back of this self-mailer lists the contents of the seminar (reasons for coming). The first inside panel has a personal message (in letter form) from the sponsor, a well-known authority on the subject. Another panel contains photographs and biographies of the speakers. Still one more panel has its testimonials from attendees in other cities. And finally, the panel with a registration form.

Effective?

Yes, which is why this is a standard form to bring thousands of attendees to conferences and seminars all over the country.

• *Food for Thought*. Ever stand in line in a supermarket behind someone with a whole fist full of coupons? Where did all those coupons come from? Many were part of a circular sent as a self-mailer to the many people with the same last name, "Occupant."

• *Mail Sail*. Ken is an ardent boater. His late August mail brings him an abbreviated catalog from his favorite marine supply house. See the bold headlines announcing end-of-season closeouts! Read all about the marvelous products you wanted to buy but could never afford. Now . . . buy!

No envelope to open. No putting it aside to find out (too late) what's inside. Everything is out front, bare, pictures, prices, and the convenience of a telephone call to make Ken's boat the best looking boat on the bay.

The main point: remember that mail is a many-splendored thing. There are all kinds of ways to capture the customer's attention and have them read, re-read and re-act.

Not the least of which is to simply let it all hang out.

CALLING CARDS: MINIATURE BILLBOARDS

Damon Runyon tells of how he was first hired by a newspaper:

"It was in Denver. I went to the editor's office and told the office boy I was there to be interviewed for a job. About 10 minutes later the boy came back and said, 'He wants you to send in your card.' Runyon had no business card. But he reached into his pocket and pulled out a deck of cards. From the deck he carefully pulled out an Ace and said, 'Give him this.'"

He got the job.

Calling cards also get the job today. They are really miniature billboards telling people who you are, what you do and how to contact you in as few words as possible.

In our seminars we have a section called "Four-Mula for Success" and talk about using calling cards as Four Contacts A Day.

Everyone meets four people every day. Think about it. As a businessperson you constantly meet buyers/sellers/manufacturers/ retailers/ businesspeople and consumers. The waiter or waitress.

The ticket taker at the show. The new people at a party. The ones you are introduced to by friends. Do you give them each a card?

"Everyone knows what I do, Murray," said our insurance salesman. "I've been selling insurance in this community for 20 years. Everyone knows who I am and what I do."

Really, we asked. And then told him he was suffering from the Curse of Assumption. He ASSUMED everyone knew who he was and what he did. But how about the fact that 20 percent of his prospects change their address every year. Some are born. Some die. Some move into town. Some move out. And he's walking around thinking "Everyone knows who I am and what I do."

Wrong. If he simply gave out calling cards whenever he was in a group setting he would be amazed how many people he knows will say, "Oh, do you sell insurance?"

Here are seven rules on using calling cards to increase your business:

1. *How to tell if your card is successful:* Does the person receiving it look at it and say, "May I keep this?" We always reply to that question, "No. I only made one. Please give it back to me... ." (Yes, yes, they keep it.)

2. *Make it relate to your business.* When Robert Burchmore, vice president of First National Bank of Winnetka drops his calling card he says, "People break their arms and legs racing to pick them up." Here's why: The card looks like a $5 bill folded in half. And when you pick it up and open it, there's Robert's name, title and bank. Gotcha!

Hartman Leather, maker of quality leather attaché cases prints their calling cards on leather.

Our local glass man prints his on see through vinyl.

Our salesman of paper bags has his calling card tucked into tiny paper bags.

Bell Paper Box from Sioux Falls, South Dakota, hands out a die-cut box. Put it all together and you see their name, address and telephone number on your just-made box.

American Sign and Indicator (the folks who make those time and temperature signs) have a calling card showing the temperature. Tilt it slightly and the temperature changes to ... the time.

Our favorite one on matching the card to the person is from Christina Eriksson, Swedish advertising consultant. On the back of her card: "Women are born leaders. You have just met one."

Allan Katz runs a direct marketing business in Memphis and has a calling card that looks like a miniature business reply card. On the back are "Most Important Telephone Numbers." Allan lists the phone numbers for President Bush, former Prime Minister Thatcher, the Pope, former Secretary Gorbachev and his own (in boldface!).

3. *What's on the back of your card?* Watch what happens the next time you give out a card. The person looks at it and then turns it over and you have nothing on the back! Why? Why not some offer?

Stew Leonard gives out his card from his world-famous supermarket and the back of it is good for a free ice cream cone in his store. Most Japanese calling cards have directions how to find their place in Tokyo on the back of their calling card. Just hand the card to the taxi driver and he'll know where to take you.

We once criticized friend, speaker, author, marketing guru Jeff Slutsky because he had nothing on the back of his card. Back came a new card from him a few weeks later. On the back was the message: "Rent this space."

4. *Make it unusual, memorable.* When someone asks comedian Henny Youngman for his card, he hands them a standard size business card with only two words on it: "My card." When they look at him surprised he says, "Didn't you say you wanted my card? That's it!"

Brill's men's shop in London has a tiny calling card. When you read it and turn it over, there is a message on the back that says, "The size of this card is made necessary by the amount of business you've given me lately."

If your next travel takes you through O'Hare in Chicago you might meet a taxi driver called Chubby who gives you his card that says:

```
For O'Hare
Call Chubby
The Man With The Plan
One day in advance.  Air Conditioned.
Treats.  Coffee.  Danish.  Stereo.  Fun.
Call and wait 15 seconds for a returned call.
```

And then this kicker at the bottom:
This card will self-destruct in 5 seconds.

5. *Spread the word.* In our banking seminars we always ask the question, "How many of you have banks where the tellers have business cards?" Few, if any, raise their hands and we then add, "Right. Don't give them to the tellers. They may give them out to friends and relatives who will then know about your bank and come to you for financial products and services. Make sure you make them for to the CEOs and and junior officers who will give them to the CEOs and junior officers of OTHER banks."

We still like the cards made up to fit your Rolodex even though Rolodex cards do come in different sizes. One of the best we saw recently was from Dunfey Hotels that ran full-page ads on the back of business publications with a dotted cut-out line around THEIR Rolodex calling card with the headline: "Give this ad to your secretary."

6. *Use color.* A simple black-and-white calling card is simple. Good for undertakers, but not memorable. It doesn't cost any more to have your card printed color on color. And it works better. Well, except for the time a banker met me at a seminar and said, "I've tried color on color for my calling cards, but I have a new black-and-white card that attracts the most attention of any card I've ever used." "Really? I find that hard to believe," I said. He gave it to me and walked away. I read and then understood why he received such a strong reaction. For there, in the middle of the card under his name and address was his made-up slogan: "Our competitors are a bunch of bastards." No, he doesn't work there anymore.

7. *Make it unexpected.* The butchers who work for Hannaford Brothers supermarkets in New England have personal calling cards they give to customers. Want your meat cut or trimmed a certain way? No problem. Call the butcher and he'll have it ready/waiting for you when you arrive.

Stamats is a printer in Cedar Rapids, Iowa, that uses the slogan, "The Hungry Printer." The front of their card is die-cut and looks like someone took a bite out of it!

Our favorite calling card story: A stockbroker we know drives to Manhattan every day. As he approaches a toll gate on the super highway he positions his car, whenever possible, in front of an expensive car — a Mercedes, Jaguar, Lexus, Infiniti.

He then hands a $1 bill to the toll collector who gives him back the change. Our friend said, "Please take out for the car in back of me as well." And the toll collector says sure, fine.

When the owner of the expensive car stops to pay his toll, the collector says "It's OK. It's already been paid."

"Paid? By whom?" asks the driver of the car.

"By the guy who was in front of you," said the toll collector.

"Who is he?"

"I don't know, but he left me his calling card."

The driver of the expensive car takes the card, turns it over and on the back reads the handwritten phrase, "If you think this is unusual, you ought to see the way I sell stocks and bonds."

For more information on calling cards, their history and size, drop a line to co-author Ken Erdman who wrote an in-depth column on this topic recently. Ask him to send you a copy. Write Ken at The Three Marketers, 402 Bethlehem Pike, Philadelphia, PA 19118.

TOOLBOX

Self-Mailers:
Styles & Folds

On the next few pages are some examples of the most often sent-through-the-mails self-mailers. We've given them names (our own) and short descriptions of what they are and how they work.

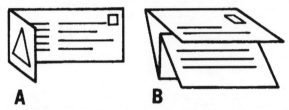

A   **B**

A. The Corner Fold: Only a part of the card is folded. Make sure the copy on the card exposed reads by itself. When the fold-over piece is laid flat you should still be able to read the entire message. Not half sentences or parts of words.

B. The Tuck-In-And-Over: This gives you a chance to capture the reader's interest as soon as the card is lifted. And/or a good spot to say, "Stop! How many of these questions can you answer?" And it becomes the back of a reply card where you have the customer now involved.

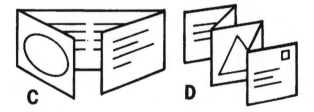

C   **D**

C. The Split Definitive: Gives you a big panorama look across all three folds when it opens.

D. The Accordion Fold: Good for providing enough room when you have several stories to tell. Each one has its own space.

E. Tuck In & Over: Good layout for lots of copy. Also serves well as a business reply envelope for one part and a message for the other.

F. The Side Arm: When you open this one, the narrow side pieces should be a different color to announce an important feature.

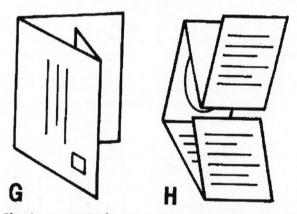

G. The Classic: A simple 6" x 9" or 8½" x 11", folded in half. Easy to read, inexpensive to print. Understood by the reader.

H. The Shuffle: This mailer is meant to entertain and hopefully not confuse. There are many ways you can open this piece so each message must be able to stand alone.

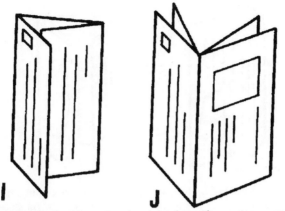

I. The Horizontal/Single Flip: Good style to have the customer open and read an important message on the facing page that explains what they are about to see on the double page coming up.

J. The Double Classic: Same as "G". Just another section added.

K. The Triple Split Definitive: The same as "C." Only three times as much.

L. The Vertical Single Flip: The same as "I." Only turned around.

M. The Double Peak: A little clumsy in handling but opens to a big finish. Good if you want to show a giant photograph.

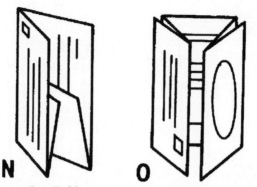

N   **O**

N. The Presentation Fold: Just like a brochure from a company. Only much simpler. Can use to tuck in ads in the folds. Many department stores do this as a mini-catalog.

O. Double Gate: Like the name says. There are two ways to get into this message.

P   **Q**

P. The Claccord: Our contraction of the Classic Fold combined with the Accordion Fold.

Q. Over & Under: Good style to use for a die-cut to tease the reader into what's waiting for him if he keeps on reading.

These are just a few of the many variations of folds you can make. Combining one with another (like the Claccord) gives you an even greater variety.

Important: Check with your printer so he can tell you what his folding machine can (and cannot) do. The machine only folds in certain mysterious ways. Work with what is available.

10

WHAT TYPE ARE YOU?

WE RAN AN AD in the newspaper every day, always in the same position.

The typeface was always the same. Typefaces have names like you and me. Sometimes it's the name of the person who designed the type face: Benguiat, Lubalin, Goudy. Sometimes it simply matches what the typeface looks like.

Futura looks futuristic. **Jenson Oldstyle** has a, well, oldstyle look.

The typeface we used in our newspaper ads was called Garamond, the same as what you're reading right now.

One day we ran our regular store ad using the Garamond typeface. We were advertising boy's jackets on sale.

Good ad. Except the newspaper left off the name of our store!

We called up our ad rep and complained. He apologized and said they would run the ad again at the end of the week, with our name, at no charge.

Fine. But it wouldn't help us sell the sale jackets that day.

Except we sold thirty-five *that day!*

We waited on the last customer ourselves. She asked to see the jackets on sale. We showed them and she bought one. Before she left we asked how she knew about the sale. "I saw your ad in the paper today," she said.

We quickly grabbed a copy of the ad and showed it to her, "But it doesn't have our name in the ad!" we said.

She examined it very carefully then looked up and said, "In *my* paper at home . . . it has your name."

What was she saying?

This: She knew it was our ad because it "looked like" our ad. *Because the typeface we use gave our business a simple and recognizable identity.*

Since type is better shown than explained, we have some illustrations in the TOOLBOX at the end of this chapter. But for now, let's list Ten Commandments for selecting type for your direct mailer:

COMMANDMENT 1. *Type has a first impression.* The book *Dress for Success* by John T. Malloy says there's a strong relationship between how you look and how you succeed.

Your business "look" extends beyond the facade of the building and the design of the interior. There is an instant identification the customer makes when he first sees your mailer. What your mailer looks like is what forms that impression. And what "type" you are is determined by what typeface you use.

That's one advantage type has for you: *type helps create your identification.*

Do not let the printer set your ads and direct mail in any type he wants. *You* pick and choose what *you* want and tell him. Otherwise your ad becomes everyone's ad or worse, somebody else's instead.

Just as your name of your business is easily recognized by your logo or symbols, so is your advertising. The eye is a creature of habit. It remembers what it has seen before.

You take your three-year-old child out for a ride in the car. She points to a billboard and says, "Look, Coca-Cola!" Can she read at three years old? No. What she saw was a "picture" conveyed by the way the Coca-Cola script appears.

The child "knew" what it was . . . because of the type. Reason why: The eye recognizes *shapes* more than letters. (See serif vs sans serif in the TOOLBOX section).

COMMANDMENT II. *Type has personality.* Some are fat. Some are skinny. Some are tall. Some are short. Some are masculine. Some are feminine. Some are plain and some are fancy.

Choose a typeface that you think "looks like" your business. Show different typefaces to friends, customers. "Which one do you think looks like my business?" You'll be surprised how many will choose the same one. (We have included some commonly used styles in the TOOLBOX at the end of this chapter.)

COMMANDMENT III. *Type has sound.* It translates how you want to talk to your readers. The big bold headline is a shout. The small type is a lot of white space and a whisper. Type can have an upper class accent or be contemporary slang.

COMMANDMENT IV. *Type creates a mood.* The local discount store has one typeface look, the department store still another and the sophisticated specialty shop yet another. Each typeface would not work if used in place of another.

That is one of the tests. Does the typeface look as though it belongs to your business. Does it have the "feel" and the "look" of who you are. Remember, you must have a look before you have an image.

COMMANDMENT V. *Type must be readable.* There is a typeface called Times Roman still used by the London Times newspaper. Today it used by more than 70 percent of the newspapers in the English-speaking world. The reason: it *is easy to read.* Next point: Make type big enough to read. There are now more senior citizens in the U.S. than teenagers.

COMMANDMENT VI . *Type should be background music.* Every movie you see has music. The purpose is to heighten your interest and hint at future developments. But the most effective background music is *not* noticeable. It creates an atmosphere but is not recognizable by itself. And so it is with good typefaces. They help to create the mood and interest but do not call attention to themselves.

COMMANDMENT VII. *Type faces should rarely be used in reverse.* That means white type on a black background. The reason not to use this style is that it violates Commandment V.

COMMANDMENT VIII. *Type should be a close-knit family.* Keep out the *relatives*. Many direct mail pieces use a half a dozen or more different typefaces. This makes the message confusing and difficult to read and follow (and buy from).

COMMANDMENT IX. *Type should have breathing room.* Leave enough white space between words and especially between lines. Make it easier for the eye to read your message. Lookhowmuchmoredifficultitisto read this. Is there a rule for the proper space? Sure. Whatever looks good to you. Experiment and see what a big difference a little space can make.

COMMANDMENT X. *Type must stand alone to be individual.* Do not set type on top of a tint or texture or a color. It will not stand out clearly. It will not be read. And the merchandise will not be bought.

Most important of all: Type is simply communication. It is the translation of how you want to talk to your readers.

TOOLBOX
TYPECASTING

In the little more than 500 years since Gutenberg printed his Bible in the mid-1400s, nearly 10,000 different typefaces have appeared, each with its own name. The one you are reading right now is called Garamond.

Originally, italic typefaces resembled the handwriting they replaced. Roman faces were based on inscriptions chiseled in stone. Soon designers began to construct their own type styles, using their own names for identity.

In 1734, a graphic artist in England named William Caslon, designed his first type. The style was so popular it was introduced in the American colonies by Benjamin Franklin and chosen by a Baltimore printer for the first official copies of the Declaration of Independence.

Today there are hundreds of type faces. Each has a name and a personality. And each comes with a complete family. (That means they usually come regular and bold and lightface. Which is how thick or heavy they appear on paper.)

Typefaces not only have different names but also come in different sizes. In type language, there are 72 "points" to an inch.

Most type comes in sizes from 6 to 72 points. Some type goes up to 120 points (see headlines on tabloid newspapers.) The larger the number, the bigger the type. What you are reading right now is 11 point. The size of the type in the classified ads in your local paper is probably 6 point.

When typesetters talk about type, they have their own language and definitions. When we talk about how wide something is we think of inches and feet (if it's *real* wide). The printer talks about picas. One pica is 12 points. Translation: A line of type 4 inches wide is 24 picas.

<small>This is 7 point type.</small>

This is 18 point type.

Type larger than 14 point is usually display type, used for headings and base lines. Body copy is set in smaller sizes. Most type comes in light, medium, or bold face (the weight of the type).

Is there a right type size for your mailer? Not really. Just big enough to read. (At least 8 point, 10 point is better.) Newspaper layouts are often as follows: The headlines are at least 24 point, the body type is 8 to 10 points. There *is* a relationship between the size of the type and the length of the line. Guide: 35 to 40 characters to a line (each space and letter is a character) is easy to read.

SERIF VS SANS-SERIF

Serifs are the little "hooks" you see on the edges of letters. This book is set in serif type because the little "hooks" or strokes on the bottom of the letters give the letters "shape" and make them easier to read.

Many of the newer typefaces are sans serif, as explained and set in the next paragraph.

More modern type faces are referred to as sans serif (without the strokes). This is fine if the type is set big enough like this.
But difficult to read if printed too tiny like this.

Final Note: Type manufacturers publish books on typefaces. Newspapers have their own type books. So do printers. Call your newspaper and printer now. Ask each of them to send you a book of the different typefaces they carry so you can decide what "type" you are or want to be in future mailers.

Here are some examples of different typefaces we commonly use.

Avant Garde

abcdefghijklmnoprstuvwxyz
ABCDEFGHIJKLMNOPRSTUVWXYZ
abcdefghijklmnoprstuvwxyz
abcdefghijklmnoprstuvwxyz

Garamond

abcdefghijklmnoprstuvwxyz
ABCDEFGHIJKLMNOPRSTUVWXYZ
abcdefghijklmnoprstuvwxyz
abcdefghijklmnoprstuvwxyz

Helvetica

abcdefghijklmnoprstuvwxyz
ABCDEFGHIJKLMNOPRSTUVWXYZ
abcdefghijklmnoprstuvwxyz
abcdefghijklmnoprstuvwxyz

Optima

abcdefghijklmnoprstuvwxyz
ABCDEFGHIJKLMNOPRSTUVWXYZ
abcdefghijklmnoprstuvwxyz
abcdefghijklmnoprstuvwxyz

Palatino

abcdefghijklmnoprstuvwxyz
ABCDEFGHIJKLMNOPRSTUVWXYZ
abcdefghijklmnoprstuvwxyz
abcdefghijklmnoprstuvwxyz

Park Avenue

abcdefghijklmnoprstuvwxyz
ABCDEFGHIJKLMNOPRSTUVWXYZ
abcdefghijklmnoprstuvwxyz
abcdefghijklmnoprstuvwxyz

Times

abcdefghijklmnoprstuvwxyz
ABCDEFGHIJKLMNOPRSTUVWXYZ
abcdefghijklmnoprstuvwxyz
abcdefghijklmnoprstuvwxyz

11

SHOW YOUR COLORS!

WE ONCE HAD an insurance agent who loved the color orange. He used the color orange in his advertising. The morning mail would always have a stack of white envelopes. If there was an orange envelope, we would say, "I wonder what my insurance agent is writing me about today?"

He wore orange ties. And carried a pocketful of little pieces of orange candy he would hand you on the street, at a meeting, at a luncheon or dinner. The local children's hospital regularly received a crate of oranges from him.

And then the day came when a young woman opened up a dress shop of her own in our town and painted the front door orange. And the citizens of the town would walk by and say, "How about that . . . an insurance agent opening a dress shop . . ."

That's what color does.

It identifies you. Your store. Your product. Your merchandise.

Once you decide on a color for your business use it all the time. The colors for our store were gold and dark green. (It's also the colors for Polo and Gucci and if you mixed us up with them . . . that was O.K.)

Quick now: What's the name of the chocolate candy with the chocolate and white letters?

What's the name of the soup in the red and white can?

What mouthwash is green?

What toothpaste is multicolored?

See how it works? You associate a color with a product.

And so, folks, what color is *your business?* Is there a specific color which, when seen, brings the name of your business to mind? There should be. And when you do your direct mail pieces you can incorporate your colors into your mailing piece.

Pay attention to color. It *will* affect your mailings. It will make a difference in whether or not your mail is read, paid attention to and (most important) acted upon.

What do colors do? They soothe. They excite. They activate emotions.

And since emotions are only a half-step away from buying (or *not* buying), let us review colors and what they do and don't do.

Men seem to respond best to earth tones: the nature colors, the browns, rusts, grays, greens, blues.

Women seem to respond best to softer colors. Pastels, pure white, shiny black.

Blues and greens are genderless. They seem to appeal to either sex.

Colors also convey a meaning. Red can mean embarrassment (blush), a country (China), evasion (herring), delay (tape), or stop (light). White can mean Broadway (Great White Way), purity or the hats the Dodge boys used to wear.

Blue can mean a nursery rhyme (Little Boy), a painting (boy), a killer (beard), or sadness. Pink can be a state of health or a sign you are out of work. Green can be envy, inexperience, a sign to go or the pastures to lie down in. Yellow is a taxi, a coward, a sign of caution, or a ribbon tied around an old oak tree.

Gold is silence, not all the glitters, the fleece sought by Jason or the rule to guide your life. (To which our local financial expert said the Golden Rule for bankers is simply: "Those that have the gold, rule.")

Gray does seem to connote conservatism and age from the flannel suit of the same color to Geoffrey Beene's cologne of the same name or the time your mirror suggests a change to Grecian Formula.

Sometimes colors become positively chameleon from the well-known horse (the one of a different color) to the panther that was a black civil rightist, a pink detective, and a grey senior citizen.

Colors can also be one word descriptions: rust (wears out); lemon (bad wares); raspberry (wherever you're criticized).

Artist Eloise Barnhurt says, "Red is the color of sex and yellow is a nerve energizer that keeps us awake." And it is true that blue connotes truth, wisdom and loyalty.

Here are some facts about color:

Fact: You *can* increase mailing results with a wise choice of colored paper and/or colored ink.

Fact: Colored stationery and envelopes outpull white stationery and envelopes.

Fact: For every test that tells you one color pulls better than another, there is another test that tells you the reverse is also true.

Fact: When everyone who reads this book convinces everyone else to use color in the mailings, the one remaining person using black and white will probably achieve the best results. Because his envelope will be the only white one in that mail.

Fact: Red and purple mean "action." Good colors for sales.

Fact: Adding a second color will increase sales.

Fact: Adding a third and fourth color will not necessarily increase sales. *(Exception:* Food. Clothing. Furniture. And then, only if the color reproduction is excellent.)

Fact: Your personal color favorite is probably the wrong one to use for a second color. What color reflects your store, your business?

Fact: Less is more. Famous architect Mies van der Rohe had it right when he said the less you use, the more dramatic the results. Picture a page chock full of red color. Picture the same page in black and white with a single dot of red color. Which page attracts your interest more?

Fact: Order or reply forms printed in colored ink and/or colored stock will outpull order forms printed in black ink on white stock.

If colors set off predictable emotional reactions (they do), why not adapt and adopt the positive reactions for your store or business (you should).

When you associate your business with an established positive color, you have taken a giant step toward bringing your customer to read what you write and buy what you sell.

Any doubts you may have as to the success of this philosophy will disappear after the next rainfall. Simply look into the sky and see the rainbow (which is all colors) and you will remember what awaits you at its end.

TOOLBOX
SPECIFYING COLOR

Most printers not specializing in color normally have their presses running black ink. A different (standard) ink color is usually no more expensive, but you might have to pay a small charge for a press "cleanup" to change to your color.

Most color specifying for printing is based on the commercial system devised by Pantone, Inc., and the system is referred to as the PANTONE* MATCHING SYSTEM. There are eight PANTONE Basic Colors plus PANTONE Black and PANTONE Transparent White, from which all PANTONE Colors are made. The formulation of colors depends on the percentages of each of these PANTONE Basic Colors used.

To standardize color specifying, Pantone publishes a variety of color guides and reference books, each with hundreds of possible color combinations shown on coated and uncoated paper, along with PANTONE MATCHING SYSTEM identifying numbers.

Each additional color of ink adds to your printing bill but there are ways to give the effect of different colors without actually changing the basic ink used. You can use papers of various colors to create a two-color look. Some colors, however, do not overprint on other colors satisfactorily.

Screens or tints of the colors selected produce lighter versions of the ink used (again, shown in color specifying references) and give you a two color effect without two-color cost.

If you are printing both sides of your paper, you can have stock

* PANTONE is a trademark of Pantone, Inc., 55 Knickerbocker Road, Moonachie, NJ 07074

with one color on one side and white on the other.

When planning a mailing piece, consider how it will be folded. With some folds, color on one side will show up, when folded, as color on two sides.

Four color (full color) printing is expensive but often necessary in direct mail packages, particularly for the brochure or selling piece accompanying the letter. This needs printers with the right equipment and experience to do a satisfactory job. The do-it-yourself concept simply requires a basic understanding of the color printing process.

CUTTING COLOR COSTS

Here are a few suggestions that will often make color more affordable than you would think.

Plan your printing time to coincide with jobs your printer may be running using the same color you want, or, find out what colors he may be running that would be satisfactory for your job.

Exact color matches add to cost. You may find a standard color that is satisfactory.

Specifying large areas of color coverage on a sheet adds to your cost.

Bleeds — carrying color to the very edges of the printed sheet — adds to the cost.

Some printers, particularly postcard printers, gang-run full-color pieces, usually on both postcard stock and coated stock. By having your piece done with others, you can greatly reduce the price of full color.

Although some artists may not fully understand the use of color in selling, they can be very helpful in getting your concept onto paper in a form that can be properly handled by the printer.

Work closely with your printer and well in advance of your needed date. Chances are your printer can offer additional suggestions that will save both time and money.

12

THE ENVELOPE, PLEASE

QUESTION: When your customers receive their morning mail, which envelope do they open first?

ANSWER: The one that captures their attention. A pile of white envelopes is nothing more than a pile of white envelopes. If one is an odd color, you pause, look again. If one is mailed from a foreign country, you pause, look again. If one is a different shape, you pause, look again. If one has a strong message on the outside offering a personal benefit you pause ... and look again.

We call this the Pause that Catches.

In a split second or two, your customers must be convinced your letter is more important than all the other letters they received in the morning

It all begins with the envelope.

And if you ask, "What about the secretary who *first* sees the mail," the answer is the same: How do you have the secretary pause and catch her attention?

People who send out direct mail know this works, and there is a continuing game of can-you-top-this in clever, different and unusual envelope designs. These are done through a difference in shape, size, style, color or texture of paper.

The trap here is you can become so clever in doing something different that everyone simply says, "My isn't that clever"... and moves on to the next white envelope with a message *they* want to read.

So the opening rule for the envelope opening is it is not enough to be simply clever. You must also have something to say *that the reader wants to read.*

This "something to say" can be actual words or a "look" that makes someone react immediately as they would if a telephone rang in their office.

How do we have the envelope be a ringing telephone?

Obvious ways: a Federal Express package. Or a Telegram. These are all loud alarms that make the reader pay attention. They are effective. But expensive.

In this chapter we will give you ideas about envelopes, how to make them interesting and eye appealing and how to create a desire to be opened by the consumer/customer/prospect.

Bill Jayme puts together one successful mailing package after another with his designer partner, Heikki Ratalahti. Here's what he says about envelopes.

"We spend about one-third of our time putting together the outer envelope. Sometimes we will use an eye-catching graphic. Or a single word written large. ('**Damn!**' read a bold display for a business magazine!) The word '**Free!**' often appears in a window cut-out to have the reader open the envelope.

"The envelope is the display window in the department store," says Jayme, "the sleeve on the record album, the hot pants on a hooker."

Jayme suggests you ask yourself three key questions when you finish putting together the envelope for your direct mailer.

1. Does your outer envelope ring the doorbell loud and clear or just timidly knock?

2. Does your package look and sound like your product? Or like every other product?

3. When the prospect receives your package is there a quick intake of breath, a delight ... or a yawn?

SIZE

What's Better: Being in Shape or Being Out of Shape? Well, It Depends ...

Envelopes, like people they go to, come in different shapes and sizes. Your choice, as a business person, should be limited to the more traditional sizes. Those you have in your drawer or your printer has in stock. There are usually three basic sizes. The small envelope (called the 6 3/4 commercial, which measures 6 1/2" x 3 5/8"), the big envelopes (called #10, they measure 9 1/2" x 4 1/8") and the 9" x 12" envelopes to mail papers you do not want folded.

As a business person, you can work with all three of these and have dozens of ways to make them not only more interesting and more readable, among the many envelopes that arrive and survive.

Each of the three basic envelopes can have a closed front or a small see-through window, through which the customer's name appears.

THE WINDOW ENVELOPE

This type of envelope has the advantage of not requiring typing the customer's name twice (once on the letter, again on the envelope). But the window has the disadvantage of not being a message that is close, personal, one-on-one. Which is why you see windows used so often by banks, insurance companies, government agencies. They have an "official" but **distant appeal.**

THE DOUBLE WINDOW ENVELOPE

One of the windows has your name and address, the **other has room** for your imagination.

It could have the return name and address.

It could be a teaser message ("Your check for $100,000 …")

It could be a stamp or a drawing or another attention-getting idea. For sweepstakes, contests, giveaways ("Bring this in to win …").

ZIP-OPENER ENVELOPES

If the key to successful direct mail is audience involvement (and it is), how do you make them become involved from the moment they receive the envelope? Here's one way: They open the envelope by pulling a tag on one side. That gets them inside and … reading.

WHAT DOES THE STATIONERY STORE STOCK?

The tan-colored kraft envelopes come in all the standard sizes described earlier but have a different "feel" and look. There are string and button closures for envelopes in stock. Or metal-clasp envelopes.

Visit the stationery store. Ask to see the different shapes and sizes they have in regular stock that are used by businesses other than yours.

What is an ordinary envelope for a different business will have an extra-ordinary look when you mail it to your customers.

ODDS TO ACHIEVE THE ENDS . . .

And how about the odd-shaped envelope or carrier for your message? Every day between 7:30 and 9:00 A.M. at your local post office, there is always a group of business and professional men and women who pick up their mail and sort it before they leave. Day after day, we watch them make a pile on the counter of the mail they will take back to the office with them. The rest they throw in a nearby wastebasket. The vast majority of this throw-away mail has something in common: it is two dimensional. The width and length may vary, but the thickness will be about the same.

See for yourself. Check your business direct mail this week. Chances are most, if not all, is two dimensional.

Recognizing the "sameness" of so many direct mail efforts two dimensional look-you'll see a simple change in size will set your piece apart from the crowd.

An odd-shaped box. An extra-large envelope. A tube. That which is different from the norm attracts attention.

And yes, costs more . . .

If you are selling a product, the question is, "Will the additional sales offset the increased cost of the package and improve overall profit?" If you are seeking leads, you must decide whether or not the extra costs have generated enough leads to reduce your cost/lead. If you are soliciting contributions, not only will the odd-shaped mailing be expected to improve the returns, but it should also increase the dollar amount of the contributions received.

If you are selling executive jets to corporate presidents, you can well afford a more expensive package. If you are soliciting funds from your local college alumni association members, the package should be unusual and/or familiar enough to make them want to read but not so expensive as to cut into profits.

The size of your audience (mailing list) also affects the economics of your mailing. Frequently, the larger the mailing, the lower the cost for the package.

Now, put yourself in the post office at 8:30 A.M. on a Monday morning. Your mail contains a tube resembling a firecracker. The copy on the outside says "Here's a dynamite idea for your next sales meeting." You shake it and you hear something inside. Into the wastebasket unopened?

Never!

TEASE FOR TWO

Should you write "teaser" copy on the outside of your envelope?

Sure. Maybe. Sometimes. Never. Of course. Are you out of your mind?

All of which are correct answers.

Sure. When you send a letter to a consumer (not an executive). This front-page headline gives them a reason to keep on reading. Wanting to know more information is legitimate, to be desired and works. *Remember:* This sentence must *always* be your prime benefit and offer. One that is instantly understandable. Or one that teases them into opening your envelope.

Maybe. If the headline offer does *not* give the reader a reason for reading and/or opening the envelope, it may do the exact opposite of what you want, and the envelope is thrown away. Make sure your outside teaser message promises a benefit or provokes curiosity.

Sometimes. Send some of your envelopes out with a message. Send some *without* a message. Code the inside return envelope or the coupon or response card so you know which pulls best. Next time use the one that worked best. But test again. Next time try a *different* message.

Never. Very personal business-to-business correspondence. Because teasers are not sophisticated, upscale, or business-looking. Too strong a sell turns many business people off. We're not talking of magazine subscription letters or seminar notices. We're talking of the important message that demands the quiet confidentiality of a plain envelope.

Of course. The envelopes with the greatest response rate, award winners (not trophies, but results) seem to be the ones with a message on the outside of the envelope. Why not copy the winners?

Are you out of your mind? An invitation to an opening of the new Rolls-Royce showroom, a letter from the Governor's Mansion or the White House. Or, simply, a personal letter from you to your customer.

THE MASSAGE OF A MESSAGE

When you visit the local health club, the masseur gives you a massage which makes you more receptive to rest and response. How do we have your message massage your reader? Here are a few ways that have worked in the past that you can adapt and adopt for your own:

Start a story. The outside of the envelope has a message that continues on the *back* of the envelope that continues *inside* the envelope. Make sure this is interesting and the customer wants to know more.

Ask a question. There is a true/false quiz on the outside of the envelope and the answer is *inside* the envelope. Curious?

Ask a question . . . then answer it! The pull up tab on this envelope is an effective reader involvement device.

Use the back. People *do* turn envelopes over. But few have anything written on the back. Give the reader *another* reason to keep on reading.

Make it personal. Yes, you can put "Private and Confidential" on the outside of your envelope because you know the message will then go directly to the person involved. But, make sure the message is "Personal and Confidential," or the angry reader will toss it aside and remember your message did *not* live up to its statement! Bad news for your future mailings.

If you are sending mail to a business executive remember that typed names outpull labels.

Make it known. Leaving *your* name off the envelope may create a certain amount of curiosity. And some curiosity seekers will open the envelope. On the other hand, there are many who will think it merely a piece of advertising mail and toss it aside. Remember one of the reasons mail is read when it goes to your customer is they know you. (See Chapter 3: The Five Ways Advertising Works.)

Your customers want to read about a product they own, the store where they shop, the newest merchandise they buy from you. So put your name out front for them to see.

The post office will cooperate with you in "cleaning" your list (making sure the addresses are accurate). Here's what you do. Put the phrase "Address Correction Requested" below your return address on your envelope or mailer. This tells the letter carrier if the person no longer lives at the address then the post office will return the piece to you *with the corrected address.* The post office will do this for about a year after the person has moved so it is important for you to "clean" your lists *at least* once a year. Put the phrase on *every* mailing so the changes do not become overwhelming at the end of every year.

There is a small charge for the post office giving you this information. It is worth the cost! Otherwise too many of your mailing pieces are simply sent to the wrong place, and the person you wanted to receive the notice does not.

TOOLBOX

Envelope Sources

Atlantic Envelope Co.
P.O. Box 1267
Atlanta, GA 30301

Automated Packaging
  Systems Inc
8400 Darrow Road
Twinsburg, OH 44087

The B & W Press, Inc.
100 Lynn Street
Peabody, MA 01960

Berlin & Jones Envelope
  Co., Inc.
2. E. Union Street
East Rutherford, NJ 07070

Boise Cascade Envelopes
72 Cascade Drive
Rochester, NY 14614

Design Distributors, Inc.
45 E. Industry Ct.
Deer Park, NY 11729

Double Envelope Corp.
7702 Plantation Rd. N.W.
Roanoke, VA 24019

Federal Envelope Co.
660 Forbes Blvd.
San Francisco, CA 94080

Golden State Envelopes
1601 Gower Street
Los Angeles, CA 90028

Gotham Envelope Corp.
100 Avenue of Americas
New York, NY 10013

Heco Envelope
5445 N. Elston Avenue
Chicago, IL 60630

Karolton Envelope
209 E. 56 Street
New York, NY 10022

Mail-Well Envelope Co.
P.O. Box 765
Houston, TX 77001

Specialty Envelope Co.
4890 Spring Grove Ave.
Cincinnati, OH 04232

Tension Envelope Corp.
19th & Campbell Streets
Kansas City, MO 64108

Transo Envelope Co.
3542 N. Kimball Avenue
Chicago, IL 60618

U.S. Envelope
P.O. Box 3300
Springfield, MA 01101

13

What's So Special About Specialties?

THERE IS A SCENE in the musical *Gypsy* where the young Gypsy Rose Lee is instructed by some of the older and more experienced burlesque professionals. "If you wanna be successful," they say, "ya gotta have a gimmick."

Gimmicks are what makes your mailer stand out — apart from and (we hope) in front of the competition. One way you can do this is with direct mail's best kept secret: the advertising specialty.

At the many seminars in which we participate, we often ask the question, "How many of you know what an advertising specialty is?"

Correctly defined, advertising *specialties* are inexpensive, useful items imprinted with an advertiser's name, logo or message, which are given out freely — no strings attached. Items given away with a real or implied obligation on the part of the recipient are known as *premiums*.

Pens, pencils, key chains and calendars are a few specialties that often come to mind. Beyond these specialties there are thousands of other items that can be used with or without imprinting to substantially improve your direct mail results. Not unlike direct mail, specialties have suffered under the "junk" stigma. They have been called gimmicks, novelties, trinkets and, worse yet, "throwaways." We'll agree that they are often novel. We'll agree that in a sense they are a gimmick. We will not, however, agree to the "throwaway" designation.

Just as we ask the question at seminars, "Do you know what a specialty is?" we also ask if the people in the audience have any specialties on their person. Almost everyone has some imprinted advertising specialty on or with them — many received in the mail.

Let's look at some of the things found among both men and women in a typical audience. There are the most common items — the pencils, pens, key chains and wallet calendars we talked about earlier — and more: a wallet-size airport directory listing all of the phone numbers for the airlines, car rental agencies and hotels in the major city served by a charter air service; a comb enclosed in a greeting card from a local barber shop; a cowboy-style belt buckle emblazoned with the word *Dallas* mailed by a trade association to attract attendees to a convention in . . . guess where?

And there were billfolds, wallets and money clips that had been mailed. Industrial companies mailed eyeglass lens cleaners, rulers and scales, pocket flashlights and screw drivers. Beauty parlors sent emery boards and nail files; retail stores were represented with sample vials of perfume. A hotel included a pack of plastic toothpicks in a mailing whose headline read, "Now you can have the pick of meeting sites."

Advertising specialties are not "throw-aways." The industry has been referred to as "remembrance advertising" or the "thank you" medium . . . and we agree. Forget the cost: it's the thought that counts.

Not unlike direct mail, specialty advertising has some distinct marketing advantages over the more popular media, including message retention, versatility and low cost. It also shares with direct mail the advantage of being a targeted and personal medium. And uniquely, specialty advertising is really a fun medium. People enjoy receiving a gift, however small, and you can "Put a little fun in your life when you put a little life in your promotions."

Now let's combine the advantages of the two media — direct mail and specialty advertising — to reap the rewards of increased returns and results.

To your typical package (the envelope with teaser copy, the letter, the brochure and the business reply vehicle) add an advertising specialty. It can be as simple as the wallet calendar or as complex as a series of items mailed throughout the year. The cost can range from a few pennies to several dollars.

Studies show that recipients believe companies that have their names on unique or substantial items are unique or substantial companies.

How does the specialty help the mailing?

1. The specialty can help get the envelope or package opened particularly if the specialty has bulk or relates to the teaser copy on the envelope. The imprinted message or logo on the specialty item serves as a reminder of the mailer or offer long after the rest of the package has been discarded.

2. The specialty can tie together the theme, the sender's name or product.

3. The specialty may be used as an element of surprise or as an attention-getter.

4. The specialty acts as a "thank you" for past business in the same mailing that solicits new business. (Remember, your *best* prospects are your *current* customers.)

The opportunities to use specialties to enhance direct mail results seem almost limitless (see TOOLBOX for 100 Ways to Use Specialties).

Here are a few case histories of direct mail campaigns used by a variety of businesses, professionals and charities which produced unusual results.

NOT-FOR-PROFIT GROUP

The local women's chapter of the Gettysburg College (Pennsylvania) alumni association traditionally mails their fund solicitation letters in early December. With contributions lagging, they switched to a February mailing to arrive on or just before Valentine's Day--and for the first time, included specialties.

The first year, a heart-shaped key tag accompanied the letter and business reply envelope, the copy on the key tag, "I Have a Love Affair With Gettysburg." Contributions increased 15 to 20 percent.

The next year, a heart-shaped cloth applique was attached to the letter and the alumnus was encouraged to wear the heart on Valentines Day. Contributions were up 25 percent over the *previous* year.

Next year: the "I Love Gettysburg" labels used by parents or students on envelopes and stationery. Results: greater increases over the previous year.

The most recent: a thin heart-shaped magnet attached to the letter by means of a special metal patch affixed to the letter with adhesive. The copy read, "Thanks for Opening Your Heart for Gettysburg." The magnet could be used to hang messages on refrigerators, desks, file cabinets and just about anywhere suitable metal was available.

Now the campaign had exposure all year long!

MANUFACTURER

Judy/Instructo was a Minneapolis-based manufacturer of children's educational toys. Every year there is a convention of the country's leading wholesalers of this product and Judy/Instructo took a booth to show their wares.

One year they had a large range of new toys. They were proud of their new, expanded line. Now, how could they attract the buyers to their booth?

They mailed each wholesaler a package a month before the show. Their theme: "We're tooting our own horn." They said they were so proud of their new items they wanted to announce the fact to everyone and included a toy kazoo in the package. They invited the customer to come to their booth, play the kazoo and win a free prize!

There were 335 wholesalers that attended the trade fair and *everyone* came to the Judy/Instructo booth. Some had practiced for weeks on special songs on the kazoo, played their number and received a prize.

A specialty sales item returned a 100 percent attendance and resulted in nearly a 75% increase in sales over the previous year's show.

INDUSTRIAL DISTRIBUTOR

A distributor of fasteners took on a new line of threaded nuts. He wanted to introduce the line quickly to his customers. At the same time he also wanted to let his customers and prospects know that he was providing a toll-free 800 number for their convenience.

His first thought was a newsletter approach, but he was willing to consider an advertising specialty.

We suggested a key ring with a portion made of plastic to resemble a round telephone dial. The number appearing in the center of the dial? His new toll-free number.

Next: A sample of one of the nuts from the new line was slipped onto the key ring and the ring reassembled. The key ring was mailed in a cloth bag with envelope attached — typical of envelopes used to mail industrial samples. The envelope contained a letter explaining the new line and listing the new telephone number with a business reply card for requesting catalogs, prices and further samples.

Additionally, a self-adhesive label showing the new number (which could be attached to a phone) was also enclosed.

Response?

"Our phones were humming with requests for catalog and pricing information just days after the first pieces went into the mail," the distributor commented. "It was probably the fastest reaction we've ever had to a new line."

CHURCHES

A church serving a middle-class suburban neighborhood wanted to reach the families in a three-mile radius to make known their various community outreach programs. The available weekly newspaper's much wider circulation posed the problem of overkill — more response than could be handled. Direct mail seemed the answer to reach a target market inexpensively. There was, however, a second problem. People might not need, or realize they need, help when they received the mailing. How could you get them to remember the services for an extended period of time?

A bent pencil imprinted with the church's hotline number and this message was enclosed:

Your life need straightening out?

For help with marital, financial, or alcohol problems CALL US!

Result: The program was quickly fully subscribed.

PROFESSIONALS

It wasn't too long ago when professionals couldn't advertise. Now that they can. Many — if not most — still suffer pangs about seeing their names in print, or worse yet, having their colleagues see their names in print.

Perhaps professionals, more than most business people, recognize that their clients (customers) are their best source of new business.

They rely on referrals. To get their clients or patients to remember them between visits and to encourage word-of-mouth referrals, many professionals have turned to direct mail . . . and specialty advertising.

New IRS rules provide both lawyers and accountants with the opportunity to mail not only the information explaining the new rules but also the means for keeping the necessary records. A wide variety of forms, booklets and diaries--all imprinted with professionals' names and addresses--were mailed to clients. When used, they provide daily ad message exposure for an entire year.

Specialties specialize in not only calling attention to a specific mailing but serve as a reminder for weeks and months after the original letter has been forgotten.

TOOLBOX

SPECIALTY
TERMINOLOGY
AND EXAMPLES

To better understand the Specialty Advertising Industry, a basic knowledge of terminology is essential since so many people tend to confuse advertising specialties with premiums, gifts and prizes.

- **Advertising Specialty** — a useful, usually inexpensive item imprinted with a name, logo or sales message which is given away freely, no strings attached.
- **Premium** — an item, sometimes imprinted, but often not, given as an inducement to make a purchase or to take some other action as part of a promotion program. It has strings attached — you must do something to gain the premium. Premiums can vary in price from under $1.00 to hundreds or even thousands of dollars.
- **Gifts** — given by suppliers of products or services to customers or prospects. They are hardly ever imprinted and vary in price, starting at about $5.00 and going as high as one wants to go. (Current income tax regulations permit deductions for business gifts only up to $25.00).
- **Prizes** — used in connection with contests. They are usually not imprinted and can vary in costs, but recipient may be subject to federal income tax for the value of the prize.

101 INEXPENSIVE IMPRINTED ADVERTISING SPECIALTY ITEMS

Address Books
Adhesive Strips
Appliques
Ash Trays
Atlas (miniature)
Badges
Balloons
Book Covers
Booklets
Bookmarks
Bumper Stickers
Business Card Cases
Buttons
Calculators (paper)
Calendars
Candy
ChartsSlide
Coin Purses
Coins
Combs
Cookbooks
Coupon Cutters
Coupon Holders
Currency Converters
Diaries
Fans
Fishing Lures
First Aid Guides
Flags
Flowers (artificial)
Fly Swatters
Games
Gift Certificates
Golf Tees

Holiday Decorations
Ice Scrapers
Insurance Wallets
Jar Openers
Jewelry
Key Chains
Knives
Labels
Lens Cleaners
Letter Openers
Lint Removers
Utter Bags
Lucky Charms
Luggage Tags
Magic Tricks
Magnets
Magnifiers
Manicure Tools
Maps
Membership Cards
Message Holders
Miniature Tools
Mirrors
ModelsPlanes
Money Clips
Nailfiles
Notebooks
Paperclips
Patches
Pencils
Pens
Phone Aids
Photo Holders
Photos

Pins
Playing Cards
Pocket Protectors
Poker Chips
Posters
Pot Holders
Pot Scrapers
Puppets, Hand
Puzzles
Rainhats
Recipe Books
Rulers
Screwdrivers
Seeds
Sewing Kits
Shoe Horns
Shoe Laces
Signs
Simulated Money
Slide Rules
Soap
Spatulas
Sponges
Sports Schedules
Stamp Holders
Stamps
Tablets
Tape Measures
Telephone Directories
Tie Clips
Tie Tacks
Thermometers
Tooth Picks

101 SITUATIONS WHERE IMPRINTED ADVERTISING SPECIALITIES CAN BE USED

(suggested by Dr. Dan F. Bagley III, Ph. D., University of South Florida, USA.)

Supplement other advertising efforts

Establish prestige

Reduce prejudices

Create corporate identity

Build broadcast audience

Spotlight favorable publicity

Make customer feel important

Obtain third party endorsements

Imply Third party endorsements

Introduce new service

Introduce new management

Serve as souvenir in gift shop

Build customer loyalty

Round out marketing plan

Serve as dealer loader

Symbolize friendship

Promote meeting attendance

Collect from delinquent accounts

Produce entertainment costs

Reward sales force

Raise funds

Commemorate special occasions

Encourage quality control

Symbolize safety effort to OSHA

Stimulate window displays

Symbolize new promotional campaign

Announce marketing plans

Symbolically apologize

Discourage brand substitution

Deliver institutional message

Tell success story

Publicize company policy

Increase catalog distribution

Stimulate work-of-mouth advertising

Serve as sample holder

Produce direct sales

Educate prospects about needs

Promote early buying

Enhance direct mail response

Target message to influentials

Create new buying habits

Stimulate grand opening traffic

Reduce required sales calls

Enhance employee pride in company

Impress present stockholders

Stimulate information requests

Enhance product distinctiveness

Improve community relations

Keep company's name in buyer's mind

Encourage trial usage

Reach altogether new target groups

Strengthen brand loyalty

Give sales reps something new to discuss

Increase psychological involvement

Enlist spouse's support

Extend peak sales season

Focus appeal to a specific segment

Produce sales leads

Stimulate sample ordering
Help organize sales
  presentations
Get users to recommend
  company
Increase product usage
Spotlight product or service
  features
Attract new users
Reach hard-to-see prospects
Test pulling power on an ad
  medium
Appeal to competitor's
  customers
Promote multiple-unit sales
Improve employee loyalty
Attract new stockholders
Discourage competing
  salespeople
Boost p-o-p sales
Welcome to community
Reduce vandalism
Promote demonstrations
Encourage use of p-o-p
Project ideas for new users
Offset competitive promotions
Offset seasonal slump
Give recognition for
  achievement
Encourage opening charge
  accounts
Reduce employee turnover
Announce new phone or
  address
Celebrate anniversary
Recruitment
Promoting branch openings

Introducing new products/
  services
Motivating salesmen/sales
  department employees
Opening new accounts
Stimulating sales meetings
Developing trade show traffic
Balancing improper product mix
Activating inactive accounts
Changing names or products
Using sales aids for door
  openers
Motivating consumers through
  premiums
Moving products at dealer level
Improving client or customer
  relations
Building an image
Motivating employees
Promoting new facilities
Introducing new salesmen

PART THREE:

POSTING YOUR MAILER

The mode by which the inevitable comes to pass is effort.
— **Oliver Wendell Holmes**

14

PRESCRIPTION FOR PROFIT:
MAKE AN APPOINTMENT WITH
YOUR POSTMASTER

ONCE UPON A TIME a visit to the post office was an awesome trip. You entered a stone-cold building, spoke in hushed tones and were surrounded by pictures of the FBI's most wanted criminals. An infraction or mistake on your part could be a government offense punishable by fine or jail sentence . . . or both!

In 1970, the United States Post Office became the United States Postal Service. Everything changed. A quasi-governmental agency behaved more like a business than a government agency.

On a recent trip to our local post office (serves 7,000 customers), we found a modern lobby containing a display case promoting philatelic activities, a free-standing display called a "service information center," a "packaging pointers" poster, charts for fees and information, signs promoting Express Mail, racks with helpful hand-outs on postal products, and a repetitive electronic billboard with a lighted small-dots message promoting post office boxes.

Yes, there was a poster "conformity with signs and directions" that spelled out potential customer pitfalls and punishments.

> *All persons in and on property shall comply with official signs of a prohibitory or directory nature and with the directions of security force personnel or other authorized individuals. Violators subject to a $50.00 fine or 30-day jail sentence or both.*

In spite of this ominous warning sign (even retailers post shoplifting warnings), post offices are looking and acting more like the retail business they really are. They merchandise their products and services. More importantly, they are servicing their customers. This new approach could save you, the mailer, untold wasted hours and money.

Even the so-called experts in direct mail, the mass mailers, make costly mistakes that could be avoided by a visit to their local post office *before* the mailing is produced. For the smaller do-it-yourself mailer, an advance trip to the post office should be as important a safety measure as buckling up your seat belt when you get into your car.

Yes, there is printed material available from the Postal Service telling you what to do, how to do it and how much it will cost. But much is left out. Or subject to interpretation. Solution: Bring your proposed mailing to the postmaster (sometimes called superintendent) or other supervisory personnel. You gain the advice and help of experts. The post office would rather prevent problems than have to deal with them. They too believe in preventive medicine.

Here's some examples of very basic mailings. And what could (and did) go wrong.

The mailing
A self-mailer with a tear off business reply card.
The problem
The mailer was printed on paper stock too thin (or too light) for postcards.

The mailing
A store mails an envelope with a letter brochure and business reply card. (BRC)
The problem
The letter, brochure, BRC so carefully weighed was weighed on a scale that did not agree with the post office "official" scale. Or it was weighed at the wrong time. (See Ken's rainy day mailer below.)

The mailing

A business sent a package similar to the one above but included a specialty item which did *not* bring the package over the one ounce first class maximum.

The problem

The post office agreed the specialty did not add too much weight but said it *did* add too much *bulk* to permit the package to be mailed at the one ounce rate.

And then there are the not-so-common problems. We call them OOOPS mail.

THE POTATO THAT PLOPPED

A creative sales manager of a manufacturer of cloth kitchen accessories came up with a unique direct mail package to promote a new line of oven barbeque mitts. In his package he included a letter, a descriptive catalog sheet and a sample of the mitt . . . along with a potato wrapped in aluminum foil positioned in the middle of the mitt. The package was timed to capitalize on the spring selling season and was mailed in February.

Unfortunately it was during one of the most severe cold spells in years. When many of the dealers opened what should have been a really exciting mailing, they were faced with potatoes that had frozen and then thawed, with mitt and literature stained at best and downright gooey at worst.

OOOPS!

HOW TO UNSCRAMBLE AN EGG

And then there was the time Murray came up with the after-Easter promotion. He sent a plastic egg out to his customers in a cloth bag. Inside the egg there was a message about his store's after-Easter clothing sale. The package was ready to mail to 10,000 prime customers with the 10,000 messages tucked inside the 10,000 plastic eggs. The mailing label had the message, "Look what the Easter bunny left for you at Gordon's."

The day of the mailing, Murray took a dozen of the packages and gave them to some staff. He was anxious to see how they would open the eggs, what message they would read first.

Each of the salespeople opened the packages, took out the eggs, held them in their hands and said, "Thanks."

"Thanks?" echoed Murray, "Thanks for what?"

"For the plastic egg. Is this a gift you are sending to all your customers?"

"But," said Murray, "Aren't you going to open the egg?"

"Oh?" said one of the group, "does it open?"

And so Murray went to the local stationery store and purchased 10,000 peel-off dots and brought them to the printer. The printer stamped "Open me up" on the 10,000 dots. And the 10,000 packages were opened and the 10,000 eggs taken out and the label attached to each one and then re-packaged in the 10,000 bags.

P.S. The sale *was* a success but came perilously close to being a candidate for the OOPS! parade.

SOAK IT TO ME!

A mailing that Ken did (he got smart the hard way) was carefully designed to take maximum advantage of First Class weight limits. Accurate scales confirmed the weight just a hair under one ounce which allowed Ken to put a lot of material into the envelope. The promotion was mailed at the end of a rainy week in April. It was returned by the post office marked "insufficient postage." The paper had absorbed enough moisture to bring the weight of each piece over the one ounce mark.

OOOPS!

Most mailings, with careful attention to planning and detail, will make it through the post office trouble free.

Your appointment at the post office is painless (and you won't get a bill). As with any organization, personal attitudes — the staff's bedside manner — may vary. We've found however that good patients can expect excellent care in the capable hands of the United States Postal Service.

TOOLBOX

Specific Mailing
Information

Since postal regulations and rates are subject to change (and changes are planned even as this book is being written), only basic reference material is included in the TOOLBOX for this chapter.

Up-to-date information is available from your local post office supervisor. If your mailings turn out to be substantial, consider joining your local Postal Customer Council.

In addition to meetings, these local councils sponsor seminars, panels and classes. They focus on fundamentals of mail preparation, automation, Express Mail, presort first-class mail preparation and bulk mail. Many meetings feature national as well as local or regional speakers who are experts in the industry. At evening meetings you may have a special tour of the post office during its busiest hours. For a membership, call your local post office supervisor and ask for a membership application.

Two additional key sources for postal information, both free:

• *Mailers Guide,* a booklet covering basic service and procedures.

• *Memo to Mailers,* a monthly newsletter to keep you current with continuing postal changes.

Both publications are at your local United States Postal Service (USPS) or write to:

National Address Information Center
US Postal Service
6060 Primary PKY Ste. 101
Memphis, TN 38188-0001

Now, let's take a look at the different ways you can mail . . .

CLASSES OF MAIL

There are four basic classes of mail:

First Class. The basic category. More than half of the over 100 billion pieces mailed annually are first class. For some types of mail (bills, statements of account, personal letters, etc.) it's the only method legally usable.

Remember airmail? Well, it no longer exists as a special rate in the United States. USPS schedulers determine whether to use surface or air, depending on distance and weather.

Second Class. For newspapers and magazines with regular publication schedules.

Third Class. Commonly known as "bulk mail." Used for advertising that *must* be presorted by zip code. A single piece of Third Class mail has a maximum weight. This changes so check with your post office.

Fourth Class. Zone rated for parcels.

Special Fourth Class is a flat rate by weight for books and sound recordings.

All the above are very simple explanations because most classes also have sub-classes.

Remember: these are the ones you will use most often. Postal rules and regulations change often. So check before you mail.

Express Mail. A premium overnight delivery service which is available to many (but not all) postal destinations. In some instances where Express Mail cannot be delivered directly to the receiver, it can be delivered to the intended receiver's post office for pick up.

Priority Mail. Guaranteed two-day delivery for packages up to two pounds at prices far lower than next day mail services.

AUTHORIZATIONS AND PERMITS

Imprint permit. A permit to use permit imprints and pay postage in cash at the time of mailing may be obtained on application to the post office where mailings will be made. There is a small one-time fee as long as the permit remains active.

Bulk rate annual fee. An annual bulk mailing fee must be paid once each calendar year (due January 1st) by or for any person or organization which mails at the regular or special bulk Third Class rates at each post office where mailings will be deposited.

Business reply permit. If your direct mail package is going to include a pre-paid by you business reply card or envelope you will need a business reply permit. Check with your local post office for current rates and regulations.

Address corrections. Any of these phrases: ADDRESS CORRECTION REQUESTED or RETURN POSTAGE GUARANTEED or ADDRESS CORRECTION REQUESTED or FORWARDING AND RETURN POSTAGE GUARANTEED, must appear below the sender's return address for you to receive new unchanged addresses.

Dimensions for mailing pieces. The USPS has strict regulations regarding all dimensions of mailing pieces for all classes of mail including width, length, thickness of stock (postcards), thickness of total package and weight. Check your mailing in advance to make sure it meets all the rules.

FIRST CLASS VS. THIRD CLASS: ADVANTAGES/ DISADVANTAGES

First class mail . . .
- Has the fastest delivery.
- Requires no bundling or sorting.

But ...it is the most expensive and costs jump dramatically as weight increases.

Third class mail . . .
- Has the lowest cost per unit.
- Costs increase slowly as weight increases.

But . . . mailings must be pre-sorted and bundled by zip code.
- Delivery is the longest.
- Must have permit.
- You pay for finding out new addresses.

HOW TO MAKE SURE YOUR MAILER ARRIVES ON TIME

Start at the beginning. Making sure your mailer arrives in the post office *in time to be delivered* means making sure it is *ready* to arrive at the post office in time.

Here's a timetable to follow. And the best way to plan ahead is to work backwards. If that sounds confusing, it really is not. Because you have to have certain things done at certain times.

1. What's the date of the "happening" in your mailer?
2. What is the date you want this mailer in your customer's hand?
3. What is the date you will deliver this mailer to your post office?
4. What is the date you will have it addressed and bundled?
5. What is the date you will have it printed?
6. What is the date you will have it delivered to the printer ready-to-print?
7. What is the date you will establish what you want to accomplish and what you want to spend?

...That's the date to start from!

FACT AND FICTION ABOUT YOUR POST OFFICE AND MAIL

Fact: Sending your mail early in the day means it will arrive at it's destination earlier.

Fact: Most businesses waste money on postage. They "guess" what it should cost. So they put on too much postage. (waste of money) or too little and the mailer comes back (waste of time). Buy a small postage scale at your local stationery store. It will save you money.

Fact: "Next day" mail can arrive three days later. And be *on time* according to the post office. Here's why: You did not check the last *pick-up* time at the mailbox. If it was 5 P.M. and you mailed at 6 P.M., you lose a day. Or more on a weekend.

Fact: They respond to complaints. With more than 100 billion pieces of mail every year, something is bound to go wrong somewhere, sometime. Put your complaint in writing to the local postmaster. He will contact you (usually a phone call) with an explanation, help and advice.

Fact: First class mail is priced by the ounce. So it costs as much to mail something that only weighs an eighth of an ounce as something that weighs an ounce. Include a reminder sheet, an order blank, another offer . . . for the same postage. And/or work with your printer on using *lighter weight* paper for stationery and envelopes.

Fact: Business envelopes (#10) travel faster. Reason why: they are processed by machine.

Fact: If you're mailing first class, write it. Say so. Stamp it. Mark it. Especially on larger envelopes which are usually thought of as third class packages. Nothing wrong with writing "First Class Mail" real big on the envelope. Everyone wants to receive something that's First Class.

Fiction: The post office won't help you. Wrong. Forget the comedians' jokes. The post office will help you. Much of it is free. Ask for the booklet, *Mailer's Guide.* This answers more than you really want to know about every day questions. Their monthly newsletter, *Memo to Mailers* will keep you up to date with what's new.

One of the very best sources for what's happening in Washington, the source of all post office regulations, is John Jay Daly, President of Daly Associates, 702 World Center Building, 918 -16th Street N.W., Washington DC 20006-2993. Write him for information on his Tipsheets and many small, informative and chock-full of facts postal and direct mail brochures. Tell him Murray and Ken sent you . . .

15

Testing, One, Two, Three, Is Anybody Really Listening?

WHICH OF THESE is a correct statement?

• A successful direct mail piece is one that has a return of 2 percent.
• A successful direct mail piece is one that has a return of 90 percent.
• A successful direct mail piece is one that has a return of one-half of one percent.

Answer: All of them.

How can that be?

Simple. It depends on what you are selling.

If you send out invitations to close friends, contractors, politicians, good customers and local suppliers to attend the grand opening of your new building and, if at this grand opening, you were going to have lavish refreshments, entertainment, door prizes and gifts, you might well expect close to 100 percent response.

If you are selling mainframe computers by mail, one lead from a mailing of 10,000 that results in a big dollar sale is a success and the percentage of return was only 1/100th of 1 percent!

The basic percentage of return that will spell success for you relies on many variables including the product or service offered, the audience, the cost of the product/service, timing, frequency of mailing and the type of response you need.

Example: You buy an expensive camera. You fill out the warranty card. You mail it to the manufacturer. They sell or rent your name to a publisher who happens to have a book on how to use the camera you just bought.

The publisher can expect substantially better results from a mailing to a recent camera buyer than from a mailing for the same book to a list of photography magazine subscribers.

Similarly, a local photographer specializing in wedding photography can expect better results from a mailing to a list of recently engaged girls than from an "occupant" mailing in the area he covers.

Some products really need to be demonstrated, seen, felt, heard, to be effectively sold by mail and consequently would have a very low response rate. *The product itself makes the difference.*

The postcard from an accounting service could predictably be expected to do better when mailed just before the income tax deadline than as a general offering of accounting services at another time of the year. Timing makes the difference.

The response you want might not be an order. Perhaps you need only qualified leads for a salesperson to follow up. Or you might want to develop a refined mailing list for further mailings with more specific offers.

The type of response makes the difference.

Often, probably too often, first-time users of direct mail are disappointed with their results. They didn't meet the mythical anticipated return. And they give up direct mail. ("I tried it. It doesn't work . . .") What a shame!

A prime axiom for the direct mail user is "keep everlastingly at it." McGraw-Hill tells us the average industrial sale is made only after five calls by a salesperson. Isn't your direct mail a salesperson that needs to make a few calls to be effective?

Frequency makes the difference.

The criteria to determine what will make your mailing successful depends on how great a response is necessary to be profitable, either in terms of actual orders or an other measure of profitability.

That response is somewhere between the 1/100th of 1 percent for the computer manufacturer to 100 percent for the lavish-party giver.

HOW DO YOU KNOW IF YOUR DIRECT MAIL IS PROFITABLE?

The same way you know if your business is profitable. You add up your costs and expenses. You subtract these from your income. If the number is on the plus side, you win.

Here's how it works with your direct mail.

1. Put down how many mailers you mailed.
2. Put down how much the total mailing cost for printing and postage.
3. Put down how much business you did.

If you have that information, you can now measure the success of your mailing.

Here's an example:

- You mail 1,000 letters for your customers to buy merchandise from you.
- Your unit cost: 50¢ for each letter (postage plus printing)
- Your total cost: $500 (50¢ x 1,000)
- You receive 50 orders (that's a 5 percent return)
- TOTAL OF ORDERS IS $2,000.
- YOUR TOTAL GROSS PROFIT IS: $1,000.
- YOUR COST: - 500.

       CONCLUSION: You made $ 500. on this mailing.

This is a very, very simple example. Sometimes your budget can be much more complicated. How do you figure in bad debts? Other advertising? Financing? Returns? If your direct mail begins to become *that* complicated, think of using a computer (see Toolbox, Chapter 4) not only for mailings but also for information about your mailings.

REFINING YOUR RESPONSE

Once you establish a response rate based on actual mailings, you are ready to take the next step *testing*.

The fate of large mailers rests with testing. Before they mail millions of pieces they must be reasonably sure of their anticipated results. Fortunately there are formulas and charts based on statistics and the laws of probability that will give them help.

As a do-it-yourself mailer you often do not get concerned with extensive testing. But even the small mailer should test one or more of these important elements:

1. The product. You may really believe people are ready for this new item from you. You may find they could not care less.

2. *The list.* If you are selling an insurance program for non-smokers and you send your package to smokers you will have a bad response. Good offer, wrong list. If you are selling toys for the new baby and you mail the offer to senior citizens, you might reach a few grandparents who want to buy, but you have chosen the wrong list.

3. *The offer.* You will quickly discover if the price is too high. The quantity too large. The quantity too small. What are the product features? Size, shape, weight, material, workmanship, where made, by whom, colors, guarantee and price. The key, of course, is to simply make the readers an offer they can't refuse.

Doubleday increased their mail order sales of books when they simply changed the headline from "Buy four books for only one dollar" to "Buy three books for only one dollar and the fourth book is free!"

4. *Creativity.* Did anyone read your ad? Why? (See Chapter 6, Off with Their Heads.)

5. *The timing.* More people buy by mail in January. Perhaps it's the money received at Christmas. Perhaps it's the guilt from the gift forgotten and suddenly remembered. Perhaps it's people being home because of the weather. Whatever the reason there are millions of letters arriving in mailboxes all over this country in January from Publisher's Clearing House to *Reader's Digest* and more all testifying to the fact that this is *the* time to mail your offer.

Now . . . after you find that one letter, that one offer, that one product that captures the imagination and the pocketbook of your customer, fine. Keep on using it.

But also keep on trying, to a small section of your mailing list with yet *another* way to sell this merchandise.

Another phrase, another price, another method of payment.

Basic testing consists of establishing a control package with a known response. Now, vary the elements of the package to see if a revised version will out-pull the control. This fundamental approach eliminates the need for complicated mathematics. Your first mailing may serve as the control and subsequent mailings in their entirety may be considered the test sample.

Don Williams of Williams Air, a small New Jersey charter air service built entirely on direct mail and referrals from direct mail customers, mails 2,500 to 10,000 pieces to prospects in a 75-mile area. Each mailing serves as a test against his first effort or control. He tested lists and found some lists continually out-produce others and his business grew. Then he tested *appeal* changes. A convenience-oriented mailing out-pulled a safety-oriented mailing. He tested letters vs. self-mailers and offers of free gifts to frequent charterers vs. discounted rates. His results got better and better.

WHAT NOT TO TEST

For the do-it-yourselfer there is the danger of testing the wrong things or too many things. Many things have already been tested and proven. Typically, we know what months are best for mailing for certain businesses and appeals.

What color stamps to use is a meaningless test for the smaller direct mail user since the results are insignificant. Leave the testing of minor changes to the big mailers. Concentrate on one or more of the five variables previously listed.

KEYING YOUR TEST

When you split your mailing and test one half against another or split your mailing list to test one portion against another, you need some way to recognize the source of your response. Mailers can code their reply address by adding keys such as department numbers or persons' names, or slight modifications in return addresses.

RECORD KEEPING

Testing not only lets you know which mailing package produces the best result but also tells you why one package out produces another. The "why" factor needs to be identified and recorded.

Keep a record of how many pieces were mailed when, and the responses listed by number with the dates they were received. Attach a copy of the mailing to the tabulation sheet for future comparison of results.

IS ANYBODY REALLY LISTENING (OR READING)

Direct mail, unlike most other media, is extremely measurable. You send your advertising to selected groups. Do they open it? Do they read it? Do they respond?

How *many* respond is the ultimate test.

Combining careful preparation with testing will have your mailings opened, read, acted on. And the cash register repeatedly opened *ad profitum!*

When is the best *time* to mail? Two answers.

1. Tests have proven certain months give a better response to mailings than any other month.

2. Further refined tests prove that certain *products* have certain months that pull better.

First things first. On the next page is a chart from Direct Marketing Association (DMA) They have tracked direct mail response from month to month. This is a good starting point for deciding when direct mail pulls best:

MONTH	COMPARATIVE
January	100%
February	96.3%
March	71.0%
April	71.5%
May	71.5%
June	67.0%
July	73.3%
August	87.0%
September	79.9%
October	89.9%
November	81.0%
December	79.0%

But the Kleid Company, one of the top list brokers in the United States, says you also have to consider your business. If you're in business or finance, the three top months seem to be January, December and September. If you are selling books, December, July and January are very good. Here are some other groupings and the months they found best to mail over a five-year average:

Self Improvement: December, January, July. (Nearly half the products and services sold on self improvement are sold in these months.)

Parents and Children: January, July, December, August, February. (More than 74 percent of the results in just these five months.)

Hobbies: July and December.

Entertainment: December, January and July.

Fund Raising: September, October, January.

Note: December and January rank in the top four best months in nine out of ten categories.

What kind of a return should you expect?

On the next page is a probability list :

If the size of the test mailing list is:	and the return on and the last mailing is:	then 95 chances out of 100, return on identical mailings to whole list will be between:
2,000	1%	.55/1.45%
2,000	2%	1.37/2.63%
2,000	3%	2.24/3.76%
2,000	4%	3.12/4.88%
2,000	5%	4.03/5.97%
2,000	10%	8.66/11.34%
2,000	20%	18.21/21.70%
10,000	1%	.80/1.20%
10,000	2%	1.72/2.28%
10,000	3%	2.66/3.34%
10,000	4%	3.61/4.39%
10,000	5%	4.56/5.44%
10,000	10%	9.40/10.60%
10,000	20%	19.20/20.80%

STATE OF THE ART

The best states in direct mail response are Alaska; Washington, D.C.; Hawaii; California; Nevada; Arizona; Wyoming. The least responsive are Mississippi, Massachusetts and Alabama. These figures are from Ray Snyder, DM consultant and former sales manager of the direct mail department of *World Book* and quoted in Bob Stone's excellent book *Successful Direct Marketing Methods*.

Finally...

In testing, you should know the Reasons Why people buy. Ed Mayer, whom we've referred to often in these pages, came up with a list of 26 reasons people buy. Every time we come up with a new one we find it is already on the list ...

When you are testing your letter or offer in the mail, look it over and see how many of these reasons why are included in your mailing piece. The more you have, the higher your rate of success.

THE REASONS WHY PEOPLE BUY

1. To make money
2. To save money
3. To save time
4. To avoid effort
5. To get more comfort
6. To achieve greater cleanliness
7. To attain fuller health
8. To escape physical pain
9. To gain praise
10. To be popular
11. To attract the opposite sex
12. To conserve possessions
13. To increase enjoyment
14. To gratify curiosity
15. To protect family
16. To be in style
17. To have or hold beautiful possessions
18. To satisfy appetite
19. To emulate others
20. To avoid trouble
21. To avoid criticism
22. To be individual
23. To protect reputation
24. To take advantage of opportunities
25. To have safety in buying something else
26. To make work easier

THE P.S.

In Conclusion...

Old H.L. Hunt rarely gave interviews.

The Texas multi-billionaire kept his own counsel. He rarely returned phone calls from the media to discuss business.

One day a local radio station talk show host persuaded him to come on his program. During the conversation the interviewer asked, "What's the secret of success?"

Old H.L. thought about that for a moment and then replied. Within a few days his answer was picked from this small Texas radio station and found its way into national media coverage. Here is what he said: "There are only four decisions you have to make to be successful. Here they are:

"*One:* Decide what you want to do.

"*Two:* Decide what you'll give up to get it.

"*Three:* Decide your priorities.

"*Four:* Decide to do it."

At this point we hope you've passed step one and have decided that you *do* want to use direct mail to increase your business.

Step two is interesting (and we have never read that one before in all the How-to-Succeed books) because it says you must *give up* something to succeed: leisure time/entertainment/another possession — a sacrifice must be made to ensure success.

Step three is what you have read up to this point.

And *Step Four* is what you do after you finish this sentence ...

APPENDIX I
Tools for the Toolbox

If you've ever been involved in any kind of do-it-yourself project, you know the job is easier and better if you have the right tools.

You do not have to spend a lot of money to create a successful mail piece!

Be it a simple postcard, a letter, a brochure, a self-mailer, or even a basic catalog, there are ways you can cut costs.

We've collected some tools for your toolbox that will come in handy for do-it-yourself readers--those who will actually put together a mailing in house for delivery to the printer.

ARTIST'S SUPPLIES

For almost everything imaginable in artist supplies write or phone for a catalog from:

DICK BLICK
P.O. Box 1267
Galesburg, IL 61401
309/343-6181

ARTHUR BROWN & SONS
2 West 46th Street
New York, NY 10036
212/575-5544

TRANSFER TYPE

An inexpensive and convenient way to paste up headlines for envelopes, letters and brochures is to use transfer type. This consists of alphabets and numbers in a wide variety of type styles and sizes on clear plastic sheets. The letters can be transferred to paper by rubbing a burnishing tool or stylus. Another form of transfer type requires the letter be cut from acetate sheets and laid down with self-adhering adhesive. Information on these products is available from:

FORMAT GRAPHIC PRODUCTS CORP.
Rolling Meadow, IL 60008

CHARTPAC
Leeds, MA 01053

LETRASET U.S.A., INC.
40 Eisenhower Drive
Paramus, NJ 07652

ENVELOPE INFORMATION

Several of the major envelope makers have valuable free information available, with particular emphasis on direct mail. Refer to your local classified directory for envelope distributors who may have this material. Or write:

BOSTON ENVELOPE
31 Middlesex Road
Mainsfield, MA 02048

BOISE CASCADE ENVELOPES
313 Rohlwing Road
Addison, IL 60101

TENSION ENVELOPE CORPORATION
819 East 19th Street
Kansas City, MO 64108

WESTVACO (US Envelope Division)
Advertising Department
P.O. Box 3300
Springfield, MA

PAPER

The "look" and "feel" of your mailing makes a significant difference in readership and results. You do not have to use white paper all the time.

Like the envelope companies, many of the major paper manufactures will provide you with swatch kits and helpful literature. But ... go first to your local sources in the telephone directory. If you have no luck, write to:

APPLETON PAPERS
Division of NCR
Appleton WI 54911

THE BECKETT PAPER COMPANY
Hamilton OH 45012

FINCH PRUYN AND COMPANY, INC.
Glens Falls, NY 12801

FRENCH PAPER COMPANY
Niles, MI 49120

GEORGIA-PACIFIC CORPORATION
Hopper Paper Division
Reading, PA 19603

GILBERT PAPER COMPANY
A Mead Company
Manasha, WI 54952

HAMMERMILL PAPER COMPANY
Erie, PA 16533

MEAD PAPER
Dayton, OH 45463

MOHAWK PAPER MILLS, INC.
Cohoes, NY 12047

NEKOOSA PAPERS, INC.
A Company of
Great Northern Nekoosa Corporation
Port Edwards, WI 54469

OLD COLONY ENVELOPE COMPANY
Westfield, MA/Dayton, OH 45463

PARSONS PAPER
Division NVF Company
Holyoke, MA 01040

RIEGEL PRODUCTS CORP.
A Subsidiary of
Southern Forest Industries
Milford, NJ 08848

STRATHMERE PAPER COMPANY
Westfield, MA 01085

UNION CAMP CORPORATION
Franklin, VA 23851

S.D. WARREN COMPANY
A Division of
Scott Paper Company
Boston, MA 02101

WAUSAU PAPE MILLS COMPANY
Brokaw, WI 544417

STOCK ART

Thousands of line drawings, illustrations, borders, symbols, cover designs, newsletter formats, etc., are available to be cut out (clip art) and pasted on to your mechanical. Among the best known sources are:

ARTMASTER•ART-PAK
550 N. Claremont Blvd.
Claremont, CA 91711

DYNAMIC GRAPHICS
P.O. Box 1901
Peoria, IL 61656-1901

STOCK BULLETIN FORMS

For sales letters, announcements and newsletters you can get preprinted letters and envelopes with humorous themes done in color. All you have to do is add your own identification and message in black and white.

CARR SPEIRS
24 Rope Ferry Road
Waterford, CT 06386

A note of caution concerning do-it-yourself graphics: be careful when you borrow. There's always a strong temptation to borrow art, headlines and even photos from other publications. Remember most material is copyrighted. Borrowing can lead to legal problems. The original user probably paid handsomely for his graphics and is not anxious to subsidize your efforts.

STOCK PHOTOGRAPHS

Similar to stock art, stock photographs, either in black and white or color, can be purchased for one time use. A complete listing of almost all of the stock photo suppliers can be found in the *Photographers Market Annual,* published by Writers Digest Books, 9933 Alliance Road, Cincinnati, OH 45252. Among the major sources are:

HAROLD M. LAMBERT STUDIOS, INC.
Box 27310
Philadelphia, PA 19150

PHOTOWORLD, INC.
251 Park Avenue South
New York, NY 10010

H. ARMSTRONG ROBERTS
4203 Locust Street
Philadelphia, PA 19104

RICHARDS COMMERCIAL PHOTO SERVICE
732 Pacific Avenue
Tacoma, WA 98402

ADDRESSING AND POSTAL EQUIPMENT

In addition to addressing by computers there is other addressing equipment available. For those who may want to meter their mail or use stamps, major suppliers of this equipment are:

ECONOMAIL
1840 S. 54th Ave.
Cicero, IL 60650

JENKIN SECURITY
Suite 7, 13th Floor
77 Pacific Highway
North Sydney, N.S.W.
Australia 2060

ADDRESSOGRAPH MULTIGRAPH CORP.
1200 Babbit Road
Cleveland, OH 44117

ASDOM HASLER MAILING SYSTEMS
8 Brook Street
P.O. Box 858
Shelton, CT 06484

POSTMATIC, INC.
780 86 Ave. NW
MINNEAPOLIS, MN 55433

DATA CARD
195 Aloha Drive
Highland Heights, OH 44143

Mailing List Information

Several of the leading mailing list brokers have booklets and news letters with helpful information for direct mailers. Write to:

DIRECT MARKETING GROUP, INC.
33 Irving Place
New York, NY 10003

THE KLEID COMPANY
200 Park Avenue
New York, NY 10166

GEORGE-MANN ASSOCIATES, INC.
403 Mercer Street
Hightstown, NJ 08520

WOODRUFF-STEVENS
345 Park Avenue South
New York , NY 10166

UNITED STATES GOVERNMENT

A great source for a wide variety of information booklets of advertising and direct mail is the U.S. Small Business Administration. Write them at:

SMALL BUSINESS ADMINISTRATION
1441 "L" Street
Washington, DC 20416

Free photographs are available from most government agencies pending on the subject material needed. The Library of Congress is another source for free photographs by writing to:

LIBRARY OF CONGRESS
10 First Street S. E.
Washington, DC 20540

Ready?
Get set...
GO!

APPENDIX II
GLOSSARY

Direct Marketing has a language of its own. This glossary lists many of the most commonly used direct marketing terms.

Ironically, perhaps the most difficult direct marketing term to define and have agreement on among experts is *direct marketing*.

Direct Marketing Magazine's definition is: "Direct Marketing is an interactive system of marketing which uses one or more advertising media to effect a measurable response and/or transaction at any location."

Drayton Bird, noted English direct response expert and author of *Commonsense Direct Marketing*, defines direct marketing as follows: "any activity which creates and profitably exploits a direct relationship between you and your prospect."

Jim Kobs, author of *Profitable Direct Marketing*, states, "Direct marketing is a term that embraces direct mail, mail order and direct response. Direct marketing uses media to deliver the message: it calls for action on the part of the message recipient: and it often provides its own distribution channel."

We categorize direct marketing as "Communication designed to complete a sale or elicit a response through direct contact with an individual."

Here are our definitions of other direct marketing terms:

A-B Split Run Testing: A technique used to measure response to mail-order ads in magazines. Two versions of an ad are run on a split basis in the same issue of the magazine and keyed for identification when orders are placed.

Address Correction Requested: The endorsement printed in the upper left-hand corner of the mailing piece (below the return address) authorizing the Postal Service to provide—for a fee—the new address (where known) of a person who has moved.

AIDA: The most popular, often quoted formula for direct mail copy. The abbreviation stands for Attention, Interest, Desire, Action.

Back End: The work done to complete a mail-order transaction once it's been received.

Bangtail: Promotional envelope with a second flap which perforated and designed for use as an order blank.

Bar Code: Reply mail addresses as a series of small vertical bars for fast machine identification.

Bingo Card: A reply card to request literature from a company.

Bounce Back: The extra offer enclosed with mailings sent to a customer when you fill an order or send information.

Broadside: A mailing, printed on one or both sides, that opens into a large, single advertisement.

Bulk Mail: Also called third class mail. A quantity of identical pieces addressed to different names which are processed for mailing before delivery to the post office and mailed at reduced rates.

C/A: Change of address.

Card Decks: A collection of postcards from different suppliers for different products mailed in a co-op basis in the same package.

Cheshire Labels: Specially prepared paper labels on rolls, in fanfold, or in accordion fold, for reproducing names and addresses to be affixed by special equipment to a mailing piece.

Circulars: A term for printed advertising in any form, including printed matter sent out by direct mail.

Cleaning the List: A term for getting rid of the deadwood. Updating a list by eliminating those who are no longer customers, etc. Approximately 20 percent of all mailing list names are outdated after one year.

Compiled Lists: Names and addresses collected from directories, newspapers and public records, to identify groups of people who have something in common.

Computer Letter: A computer-printed letter which can be personalized with fill-in information. (See Personalized Letter.)

Continuity Mailing: A series of mailings to the same audience on a regular basis.

Continuity Program: Products or services bought as a series of small purchases, rather than all at once. Generally based on a common theme and shipped at regular or specific intervals.

Control: The letter or mailing which produces best in split-run testing and then is used as a guide against future tests.

Controlled Duplication: A method by which names and addresses from two or more lists are matched (usually by computer) in order to eliminate or limit extra mailings to the same name and address. (See Merge/Purge.)

Co-op Mailing: A mailing in which two or more offers are included in the same envelope, with each of several mailers sharing costs according to a predetermined formula.

Cost Per Inquiry (CPI): The total cost of mailing, divided by the total number of inquiries received.

Cost Per Order (CPO): The total cost of mailing, divided by the number of orders received.

Cost Per Thousand (CPM): The total cost per thousand pieces of direct mail, "in the mail."

Coupon: That portion of a promotional piece of advertisement intended to be filled in by the consumer and returned to the advertiser to complete the action sought.

DMA: Abbreviation for Direct Marketing Association, (6 East 43rd St., New York, NY 10017).

Data Base: Information which provides a customer profile—age, sex, job, residence, buying habits, etc.

Decoys: Coded names which are not recognizable to users of a mailing list. The decoys prevent illegal or multiple use of a rented list, since list owner monitor the list through mailings received by the decoys.

Doubling Day: A point in time established by previous experience when 50 percent of all returns to a mailing will be received.

Dupe (Duplication): Appearance of identical or nearly identical entities more than once.

Fill-In: A name, address or other words added to a preprinted letter.

Flats: Large-size, first class mail, usually weighing more than one ounce.

Front End: Activities Necessary for—or the measurement of direct marketing activities leading to—an order or contribution.

House List: Mailing list of *your* customers or prospects—not rented or bought.

Involvement Device: Something enclosed with a mailing to get the recipient actively involved with the mailing, such as a token, stamp, puzzle, pop-up, miniature pencil. Something that has to be handled

Johnson Block: A block of copy inside the border at the top of a letter, before the salutation, highlighting a proposition or the main selling points.

KBN (Kill Bad Name): Action taken with undeliverable addresses (i.e. see Nixies). You KBN a Nixie.

Key Code: A group of letters, numbers, colors, or other markings used to measure the specific effectiveness of media, lists, advertisements and offers.

Keyed Response: Adding special identification to a return address to determine the source of a response. Department numbers are frequently used.

Lettershop: A business organization that handles the mechanicals of mailings such as addressing, imprinting and collating. Most lettershops offer printing facilities, and many offer some degree of creative direct mail services.

Lift Letter: A small letter, folded, or folded *and sealed*, enclosed with a mailing which incorporates additional reasons to buy. Copy on the outside of the letter usually suggests that the letter is to be opened only if the recipient has decided *not* to buy. The lift designation refers to the letter's ability to increase results.

Lift Broker: A specialist who makes all necessary arrangements for one company to make use of the lists of another company. A broker's services may include most or all of the following: research, selection, recommendation and subsequent evaluation.

List Rental: A arrangement in which a list owner furnishes names on his or her list to a mailer, together with the privilege of using the list on a one-time-only basis (unless specified in advance). For this privilege, the list owner is paid a royalty by the mailer, "List reproduction" and "list usage" more accurately describe the transaction since "rental" is not used in the sense of its ordinary meaning of leasing property.

List Segmentation: Dividing a mailing list by various factors, such as title, type of product previously bought, size of purchase, sex, geography, etc.

Mail Order Action Line (MOAL): A service of the direct Marketing Association which assists customers in resolving problems with mail-order purchases.

Mail Preference Service (MPS): A service of the direct Marketing Association for consumers who wish to have their names removed from national commercial mailing lists. The name-removal file is made available to subscribers on a quarterly basis.

Match: A direct mail term used to refer to the typing of addresses, salutations, or inserts onto letters with other copy imprinted by a printing process.

Member-Gets-Member (MGM): A customer recommends a friend's name for you to contact, and gives you permission to use *their* name as a reference when you make the call.

Merge/Purge: The process of eliminating duplications between lists. The lists are "run against each other" on computers, and a net name results.

Multiple Buyers: A person who has bought your product two or more times. (Not one who has bought two or more items.)

Negative Option: A buying plan in which a customer or club member agrees to accept and pay for products or services announced in advance at regular intervals, unless the person notifies the company not to ship the product(s) within a reasonable time after each announcement.

Nesting: Placing one enclosure within another before inserting them into a mailing envelope.

Nixies: Mail that could not be delivered and is returned to the sender.

North-South Labels: Mailing labels that read from top to bottom and can be affixed with Cheshire equipment.

OCR (Optical Character Reader): Device which reads addresses electronically.

Peel-Offs: Gummed labels affixed to a slick surface which can be peeled off to transfer an address or token from one portion of a mailing to the reply vehicle.

Premium: An item offered to a buyer, usually free or at a nominal price, as an inducement to purchase or receive more information on a product or service via mail order.

Personalization: Employing a computer to personalize a letter by using the recipient's name in the salutation and in the body of the letter.

Piggy-Back: An offer that hitches a free ride with another offer.

Post Card Mailer: Booklets containing business reply cards which are individually perforated for selective return, used to order products or obtain information.

Psychographics: Characteristics or qualities used to denote the lifestyle or attitude of customers and prospective customers.

Pyramiding: A method of testing mailing lists in which one starts with a small quantity and, based on positive indications, follows with increasingly larger quantities of the list balance until the entire list is mailed.

Recency: The latest purchase or other activity recorded for an individual or company on a specific customer list.

Reply-O-Letter: One of a number of patented direct mail formats for facilitating replies from prospects. It features a die-cut opening on the face of the letter and a pocket on the reverse. A addressed reply card is inserted in the pocket and the name and address thereon shows through the die-cut opening.

Roll Out: To mail the remaining portion of a mailing list after successfully testing a portion of that list.

SIC (Standard Industrial Classification): A government assignment of special codes for various industries.

Split Run Testing: A method of testing a mailing's effectiveness by sending different or altered mailings for the same product to different segments of your mailing list. The mailing that produces the best return is then used. (See Control.)

Testing: The secret of success in mail. You can test price, copy, offer, charge/no charge, premium/no premium, and a number of other variables. The trick is not to test too many elements of your package at once. (Price vs. copy vs. lists all in the same test may give you not answers, but total confusion.) Structure your test simply to discover what you want to know specifically.

Thirty-Three Up: Sheets of address labels, 33 labels to a sheet.

Universe: The total number of persons who might be included on a mailing list. All of those who fit a single set of specifications.

Update: Adding recent sales and up-to-date information to the main list to reflect the current status of each customer.

Other products available from Raphel Publishing . . .

Tough Selling For Tough Times by Murray and Neil Raphel $ 19.95
Our latest book! Includes characteristics of successful business people.
Cassette companion to **Tough Selling for Tough Times** $ 9.95

Mind Your Own Business by Murray Raphel $ 19.95
Promotions that work in business. Lots of stories and ideas in this book.

Mind Your Own Business audio cassettes featuring Murray Raphel $ 39.95
Four audios with direct marketing success stories.

Network Your Way to Success by Ken Erdman and Tom Sullivan $ 19.95
Proven networking strategies.

Crowning The Customer by Feargal Quinn $ 19.95
Customer service tips from a leading Irish supermarket chain owner.

100 Ways to Prosper in Today's Economy by Barry Schimel, C.P.A.   **$12.95**
Practical & proven strategies to improve your business' bottom line.

The Great Brain Robbery by Murray Raphel and Ray Considine   **$19.95**
Steal marketing ideas that work.

Stealing The Competition video featuring Murray Raphel $ 39.95
How and why direct mail meets all your advertising needs.

Tooting Your Own Horn video featuring Murray Raphel $ 70.00
Murray's live presentation at the '92 FMI convention
telling supermarket ideas and work.
Video and workbook. $ 80.00

Three ways to order

Mail: Raphel Publishing
        12 S. Virginia Avenue
        Atlantic City, NJ 08401 U.S.A.

Phone: (609) 348-6646

Fax: (609) 347-2455

        Check, American Express, Visa, MasterCard accepted
        Add $3.50 for first item and $1.00 each additional item for shipping